Heads up MOM

The early years with **baby & toddler** are a whole lot sweeter when you know the truth

LORI ARNOLD

What first-time moms are saying ...

"Yes yes YES! I've bumbled through the early years wondering WHY THE HELL didn't anyone warn me about x,y,z?! This chapter is a gift to future readers. The tangible, real life examples. I could relate to nearly everything. [On 'Moms Can Do Hard Things']. Can't wait to have this in a hard copy to mark up and flip back to time and time again..♥" – **Stephanie**

"I found myself nodding time and time again at how similar and difficult it was to learn many of the lessons in the book as a new mom, and time and time again as kids grow and change. It helps the reader take heart, knowing they are not alone in the journey." – **Kelli**

"As women, we don't hear enough about the challenges motherhood brings. Nobody really shares about their motherhood journey so candidly and honestly. As a result, when first-timers go through any of these challenges, they end up feeling isolated, guilty, and feel as if they're doing something wrong because motherhood isn't this perfect experience they've been told about. I especially liked how the ups and downs were addressed in such a positive, solution-driven mentality. It made the whole motherhood topic a lot more approachable and less intimidating. One thing that stuck with me is to address expectations across the board with your partner, from small chores all the way to the harder conversations like disciplining a child." – **Eva**

"We had our baby girl last month! It has been a whirlwind for sure and I'm so glad I was more prepared from this book!" – **Mandy**

"This was sooo well articulated and sooo useful." [On the transition from Mr. and Mrs. to Mommy and Daddy]. – **Monica**

"This will be a really helpful—invaluable even—guide for any new mother that makes the good decision to read it." – **Melanie**

To Annie & Izzie—you light up my life, challenge me to grow everyday, and without you, this book could not have been written.

To Patty—your dedication to motherhood is one of the greatest gifts I will ever receive.

Cover design: Rosemary Strohm

ISBN: 979-8-9876251-0-1 (Paperback)
979-8-9876251-1-8 (Ebook)
979-8-9876251-2-5 (Audio book)

CONTENTS

Motherhood: The Greatest Transition

Hi, Momma!

Congratulations on your new adventure! Motherhood can be the most joyous time. Being a mom is everything. It's joy. It's growth. It's strength. It's legacy. It's love. It's a huge blessing. Being a mom is also doing things you never thought you would do. Saying things you never thought you would say. Changing in ways you never expected. Sacrificing in ways you've never dreamed. I say motherhood *can* be a joyous time. For too many new moms, however, this joy is dulled by the unexpected. In all truthfulness, motherhood knocked me flat on my face.

When baby number two came, I felt like I was starting over on a whole new learning curve paired with round two of emotional ping-pong. I was used to being an achiever; I was no longer achieving.

It was the nightly bedtime routine after one of the longer days that make up the short years of early motherhood. We said prayers, read a bedtime story, put a fresh diaper on, tracked down our favorite blankets, and hopped in bed. It was at this very point—after a day packed with cleaning, meal administration, constant supervision, teaching, and the management of a few "toddler traffic jams" (more on that later)—that an internal longing took over. Mental and physical freedom awaited me on the other side of that bedroom door.

"Just one more story, Mom?" asked my daughter. Next, she wanted me to repeat everything she said, verbatim. She had been in a phase where she needed to feel like she had some power in her little world, which was achieved through this game.

I repeated each phrase back to her: "I love you. Have a good night's sleep. See you in the morning. I love you ten thousand, trillion, million, infinity. Sweet dreams. See you in the morning. I love you. Good night." Then she needed another hug. Then she thought of one more thing she wanted to tell me. Next, she wanted water. I told her we'd get some in the morning and said goodnight. As I closed the door, she called for me again. *For the LOVE!* was all I could think. "This is THE. LAST. THING," I screamed at her in a completely frustrated, unkind tone as the last ounce of my patience slipped away. "I love you," she said.

There it was. I had ruined a precious moment full of love, and turned it into an ugly display of impatience. To an outsider, the sweetness of this bedtime occurrence rivals a good Hallmark movie. But for me at the time, it pushed me past my limit. Regular feelings of simultaneous love, guilt, and frustration was not something I expected motherhood to bring. In fact, most of my expectations were off the mark. Being a mom is awesome. It's also ridiculously hard.

The jolt of early motherhood can be attributed, in part, to unbalanced feedback we get from our baby-fogged inner circle. "You're having a baby?!" "Let me throw you a shower." "Let's have a gender reveal party!" "What will you name him?" "Do you have the nursery finished?" "Here are some adorable little onesies and precious books for you." None of this is bad. It's tremendous, actually. The blessing of a new life is one of the greatest reasons of all time to celebrate. Problem is, all this hype without a counterbalance sets up a new mom with a disadvantage from the very beginning. Our expectations are firmly planted in unrealistic soil.

Here's how this played out for me: Before our first daughter was born, I had *zero* conversations with my husband about who would be responsible for what (which is the biggest mistake any expecting couple can make—but more on that later too). Even *after* I had a handle on what the massively amplified workload looked like for a family of three, I neglected to engage him in this division-of-labor discussion. I had no idea how to treat eczema, constipation, or the plugged nose of a baby who did not yet know how to breathe through her mouth. I struggled with how to get the toilets cleaned when I had been told to "sleep while the baby is sleeping." I was on the furthest side of clueless regarding how to guide a child through developmental stages (or what those stages even were). I didn't know that keeping socks on a baby would make the new-mom "difficult" list. I didn't know that if I managed to keep them on, they would end up with poop on them at every diaper change. These are the normal challenges brought by the learning curve of any new job. But it continued.

I had no idea how challenging the circular nature of teaching children would be. I didn't know it would be impossible to keep my lips off of them. I never expected to feel such exasperation toward my children. I also couldn't grasp how deeply invested I would be in them. I cared so intensely about their well-being. This investment was attached to another enormous challenge: how to discipline my children in ways that would empower them, yet establish the firm boundaries children desperately need. I didn't realize how special it would feel to celebrate my first Mother's Day with a child of my own. I wasn't aware that I had left a great deal of my identity and personal freedom behind as I brought my daughter home from the hospital. Perhaps most significantly,

I didn't realize how much personal growth lay in front of me. I didn't know anything.

Your friends and family mean well when they "ooh" and "ah" over your pregnancy and new baby. They certainly wouldn't want to scar you with a bunch of early warnings. I have a different philosophy.

I know you can handle a scar or two (and likely already have) as you transition into the role of momma bear. I care less about boosting your dopamine levels and much more about making this life shift smoother than it otherwise will be. I want you to be able to catch the ball (or at least bat it away) rather than having it nail you squarely in the face as it did to me. I want you to relish in this blessed vocation, and I want to help by giving you a heads-up.

I've read about children's whole brains. I've read about raising resilient kids. I've spent hours learning about positive discipline and gentle parenting. I've read about sleep training, baby-led weaning, and potty training. I've learned about giving kids the gift of enough and the gift of failure. I've read about how to love my man without losing my mind and how to not hate my husband after having kids. I've studied how to become "mom strong," how to raise an adult, how to raise successful people, and how to "only love" today. I've read about the modern motherhood dilemma, and I've even heard from some moms who just want to pee alone. All of this was helpful in various ways. The resource I was sorely missing, the gap this book seeks to fill, was one that would prepare me, not on how to raise a baby, but for the new life-stage baby brings. In this world of open and endless information-sharing, I was dumbfounded that my new-mom hill climb was so incredibly steep. I had prepared to take care of my baby; I had not prepared to be a mom.

New moms deserve a heads-up. The massive life changes that baby brings along for the ride will be a melting pot of joy, frustration, personal growth, stress, hope, anxiety, and the greatest love you've ever known. I didn't understand the "why" behind the saying, "Being a mom is the hardest job you'll ever love." The awesomeness of mothering should far overshadow the hard moments. In the early years, however, many moms struggle to make this a reality. And that's just what happened with me. I struggled far too much through the first years of motherhood, and I share my stories and advice with the hopes of helping you avoid the potholes that blew out my tires. And there will be potholes.

That's why I wrote this book. Too many new moms face massive struggles due to missed expectations of motherhood. When our expectations are out of line or when normal child mishaps occur, we think we are doing something wrong, or worse: that we aren't good moms.

An understanding of what motherhood really looks like day-to-day is *empowering*. When your expectations are better aligned with reality, disappointment and frustration are put in their (certainly present, but properly reduced) place. When you face the WTF moments of motherhood, it is reassuring to know that every new mom has cleaned poop off the carpet (and the walls and the baby's hair) too.

Despite all the tough stuff I'm about to get into, know that love reigns supreme, and you already have it in abundance. Maria Shriver once said that mothering is a presidential task. It is. Let that sink in. There is no beautiful mansion, security detail, or team of chefs, housekeepers, or assistants; however, the role of a mom is monumental. Mothering is hard when you just stick to the basics of preserving the life you just introduced into the world. Add in the desire to raise God-fearing, values-driven, confident, inherently good human beings and the vastness is breathtaking. Whatever you do, know that you are going to be a great mom.

My promise: You will finish this book better equipped to tackle this presidential task.

Variations in the Journey

Motherhood is a dynamic space where both vast differences and eerily similar commonalities exist across experiences. You have a unique personal history and set of circumstances, expectations and goals, and a hard-wired personality that comes into play. This is different for every mom. Your child also has a hard-wired nature of his own, which adds additional variation to a family dynamic. A second child brings yet another personality into the mix. I've heard some people compare having a baby to playing the lottery. None of us know exactly what kind of baby we will bring home. Some are "hard," whether due to colic, a medical issue, or a "spirited personality." Some are "easy," largely happy and content no matter the situation. And some are somewhere in between. All moms will face challenges unique to their situation. All moms reading this book, however, have a lot in common. Foremost, we care. Deeply. We want the best for our kids. We want them to become good people. We want them to become well-adjusted adults who are capable of weathering life's many storms. Motherhood is new. We have instantly become always-on teachers. All moms experience the process of guiding our children through various phases of growth. We will all experience challenges to our patience, time, and yes, our sanity. My hope is that the vast majority of the information contained in these chapters will lift you up, spark some ideas, and better enable you to tackle this most important job of mothering.

What You Will Gain from This Book

This is not a how-to book about feeding, sleeping, potty training, or how to raise a specific type of child. Books on these topics are plentiful. This is a book of day-to-day realities, considerations, personal experiences, tips, tricks, and strategies to ease the daily task of mothering. This is motherhood from the front lines.

In the first chapter, I talk about unspoken changes and self-reflections that accompany baby. With this in mind, I lay out the realities of limited time and the unavoidable trade-offs related to various career considerations. I then discuss how to prepare for your now elevated partnership with your husband, who will likely experience an adjustment to parenthood different from yourself. Next, I provide a view of the future with details about the changes to expect as you move through your child's early ages and stages. I'll give you a heads-up on the unexpected things kids do, tips for guiding your child while her brain is undergoing early development, and other critical considerations to help as you write your unique motherhood story. Tips and tricks are woven throughout, but I dedicated the final chapters to nothing but rapid-fire tips and strategies to make your days better. To keep the information from being too vanilla and thus unhelpful, I provide specific advice and examples of situations applicable to many, but not all, new moms.

If you are in a committed relationship with your baby's father, consider the terms "husband" and "partner" interchangeable. Your time is precious, so if you don't plan on having a second child, skip the information on baby number two. If you don't have a husband to co-parent with, skip the chapters on how the expansion of your family just impacted your life more than his. *Take what looks like help and leave the rest.*

Before we jump in, let's ground ourselves in that which should never get lost: Being a mom is an awesome blessing.

The Amazingness of Motherhood

As you take on this incredible, forever-changing role of "Mom," it's really critical that you internalize the following: You are a blessing to our world. You have a unique set of gifts, abilities, knowledge, and experiences that not one other person has. Now, you have the awesome job of applying and passing on these gifts to your precious child in a way that only you can. You get to help her find and use her one-of-a-kind power in this world as well. How exciting is that? What you might not realize is that your growth is about to spurt right alongside your child's.

Raising a child will make you better—all the way down to your soul. You will discover a whole new stratosphere of selfless. You will become a better listener. Your patience will expand exponentially. You will boost your resourcefulness, agility, humility, sense of humor, problem-solving skills, and the ability to let unimportant things go. You will see a bigger picture and recognize how limited our control really is in this life. In doing so, you will lean on God and pray for His loving arms to surround your child as she faces more and more of the world with each passing year.

"Motherhood sparks us to grow right alongside our child."

—Lori

You will work with your husband in a way you never have before, on decisions that are of far greater importance than most you have encountered until now. Your perspective on the world and your place in it will change for the better—and the amazingness doesn't stop there. You will experience the type of pride and love that only raising a child can produce. You will feel the joy brought by carefree laughter. You will experience great happiness in witnessing your child learn to walk or draw his first picture. Your heart will melt when your son says he wants to marry you and relish in the innocence of your daughter's impromptu dance show. You will forever remember the wonder brought to her eyes in seeing a rainbow for the first time. Perhaps the greatest of all blessings is the elation you will feel upon witnessing your child demonstrate the values you have been tirelessly working to instill. Of course, you don't need a heads-up here. I just want to make sure, before we dive in to the changes, challenges, and chaos, that you understand the crucial big picture—and that you know that you are already an awesome mom. Believe it.

My hope for you is to find all the joy in the blessed vocation of motherhood, and I hope this book creates more space to make that a reality. I come from the future bearing a curated set of first-hand experiences, personal wins and losses, lessons, and encouragement, and I offer it up in hopes that your early motherhood journey will be all God has created it to be. Thank you for changing the world through your work and dedication.

CHAPTER 1

Embracing a New Life Stage

The elusive "they" say that certain life events create a "pre" and "post" effect. There's your life before, and there's an exceptionally distinguishable life after. Having a baby sits in the bullseye of this phenomenon.

For me, children have expanded my life. It was great prebaby. Yet, looking back, it now feels like I was scratching the surface of its depth and meaning. There are many incredible and profound layers to life I am only now coming to understand. The passage of time opens the gate of reflection. However, we must actually live through these moments in order to look back. The sheer magnitude of this major life transition can be a shock.

Have you ever heard of the term "matrescence?" I hadn't until years after becoming a mom. This term was coined by Dana Raphael, Ph D. in 1973 as the physical, emotional, hormonal, and social transition to becoming a mother – which include changes significant enough to rival "adolescence." It is such a shift, that a whole new term was created to help us moms wrap our head around this life stage we've just entered!

Here's a heads-up on the pieces of matrescence that took me by surprise, including changes a new baby often brings but are rarely talked about.

Time Reallocation

Remember your very first job? It was hard to learn the ropes, establish your network, and get your footing. After landing my first job out of grad school, I had dreams for weeks about my assigned brand, Zest soap.

Everything is harder when you're first getting started. In an instant, we are in new-mom orientation without the proper resume to back us up. The time, care, and concern for a baby is an all-consuming job. This makes breezy prebaby activities now a significant undertaking. Without realizing it, our personal freedom quietly slips away as we bring a baby into our life. Some common examples of things we are now legitimately challenged to make time for include:

- showering (I've never heard a new mom *not* genuinely experience this)

- drying our hair

- putting on makeup

- exercising

- meal prep

- reading

- praying

- going shopping

- socializing

- [insert your favorite hobby here]

To put it plainly, our time is reallocated—to our baby.

Pulling enjoyable activities off the field and subbing in feedings, soothings, and diaper changes leads some moms to feel lost. We lose autonomy, predictability, restful sleep, and a general sense of control over our days. Babies can wreak havoc on our lifestyle, and it can feel like grief. Some even have a very tangible experience of mourning the loss of their old self as they embrace a very different life.

Every one of us would choose this new life over the old. Still, it's a hard realization. Just like a high school graduation, geographical move, or significant job change, it's both an end and a beginning. There is a starting-over of sorts. And with it comes all the emotions of our soul's recognition that time is both irreversible and irreplaceable.

"Sometimes I think God likes to tease us. When we're expecting, we get an inflated amount of attention. After baby arrives, we seemingly disappear."

—Lori

The transition to this new stage of life is a hard shift to make at first, especially in baby's first year and perhaps even longer. Rest assured, you are not lost (or if you are, know that you will be found). This is just a phase of life where the vast majority of your time is spent providing care for another. This is an enormous change, and it is one that can be difficult to fully grasp until you experience it. The expectation I want you to set here is one of "always on." I call it mom-mode. Never in your life have you had to worry or care for something or someone without end. Along the way, you will make choices about what activities you can let go of (just for now) and what bucket-fillers you will fight to maintain.

The sacrificial nature of motherhood cannot be understood until experienced. Our culture today views "sacrifice" as a bad thing. It's not at all. Our Savior sets the ultimate example of this, enduring the deepest physical and emotional pain out of nothing but an incomprehensible love for you and me. I didn't realize this when I was younger, but *sacrifice is directly tied to love.* Sacrifice always accompanies deep, unconditional love. The love you have for your child has no boundaries. As such, you will make adjustments and sacrifices in major ways. The most significant postbaby sacrifice occurs with your time, which easily feeds into another change— your sense of *self.*

Unexpected Emotions

Newish moms can face hard-hitting emotional struggles. What is not acceptable is how few know how normal many of these weighty feelings are. Molly Millwood, psychologist, mom, and author of *To Have and to Hold: Motherhood, Marriage, and the Modern Dilemma* shines a needed light on these struggles.

She notes the common feelings many moms experience in the early years of this major life transition. Our lives can feel damaged, altered, disrupted, and disfigured. We feel boredom. Guilt. Uncertainty. Depleted. Constrained. Exhausted. Overwhelmed. As we begin to internalize the loss of our freedom, very unexpected feelings of resentment and even regret toward our baby can coexist right alongside a deep, unwavering love for him. These conflicting feelings can really throw us! And, because no one talks about it, and we only see blissful stories online of how great other new moms are doing, we feel unfit for the job. We question. We doubt. We feel a *normal* sense of grief over things we have lost, yet we believe we *should* be nothing but happy and grateful for this new baby. We feel shame. We feel ashamed that we feel grief. Hear me mighty new mom, if guilt or shame begin to creep into your motherhood experience, squash that thinking immediately. Other moms are experiencing the same challenges. They just aren't talking about it. If you want to dive deeper into the emotional changes many new moms face, I highly recommend Molly's book. Despite the challenge of adjusting to some heavy emotions and an "always on" way of living, there is much to be encouraged about.

While it may feel like your life has been put on pause, the flip side of this coin is soul-building growth. The round-the-clock care you now provide another person will spur growth. It sure did for me. It will make you more selfless, more humble, more aware of life's big picture, and certainly much more empathetic toward others. It can be hard to see these blessings when you are fogged over by tiredness and baby care, but know that God is working here.

Accepting a New Reality

I've heard some moms admit to an initial, very unrealistic thought that their child would be a side gig—that somehow their baby would blend into their current life without too much fuss. This ideal calls for a "yes, but." Yes, you should recognize yourself after having a baby. Yes, you should absolutely maintain the essence that makes you sparkle and keep those things that bring joy and are most important to you.

But, you have a baby. Babies change everything.

I get concerned when I hear expectant moms talking about how the baby will "slide right into" their current life, as is. The extent to which this can be done will depend on the temperament and needs of your child (i.e., which variety you brought home from the baby lottery); your childcare bench (i.e., those who will provide care for your child); what your prebaby life looked like; and your priorities.

Set yourself up for success by being aware that providing care for babies, toddlers, and little kids is very time intensive, whether at home or out and about. It's simpler to get up and go with easygoing babies. Still, be prepared. Packing up a child (and all their stuff), supervising, changing, feeding, and soothing tired or gassy children changes the going-out game. This holds for all ventures, whether a quick errand, trying to meet up with a girlfriend, or any kind of trip. Unless you arrange third-party care, your general mode of operating will be different.

Anticipate Mental "Tugs"

If you develop a deep roster of people who will help with childcare, you will have more flexibility to maintain some prebaby activities. But be prepared. You might experience a mental "tug" from home when you go out without baby, at least in the beginning.

You may have to deal with thoughts like these interfering with your time away from your little one:

- Is the baby OK?

- Did he eat well?

- Will the babysitter be patient if she starts screaming?

- Did he get to sleep OK?

This is super normal and will fade as you solidify your priorities and become more acclimated to third-party care. Some moms don't feel this. Others want to wait for quite a while before leaving their baby for a night out. This is completely your call to make.

Priority Shifts

Knowingly or unknowingly, you will begin to set priorities related to your newly changed way of life. I would encourage you to be intentional about these priorities. Ask yourself these questions:

- How much social or outside activity time is important for me?

- Is it a priority for me to be available to breastfeed my baby?

- Is it important to me that my child keeps a steady nap schedule?

- Is it important for me to eat real food and minimize my pantry pulls?

It's all a big game of give and take. As you begin to realize some of these changes and challenges that accompany welcoming a new member of the family, reflect on these priorities and shift them as needed. Most of all, please give yourself time. Attempting to resume normal life shortly after leaving the hospital may be an unnecessary burden.

A friend of mine planned a vacation when her baby was about four months old. She and her husband booked the flights and hotel, and got excited about their usual getaway. They packed up the burp cloths, extra clothes, pacifiers, noisemaker, blankets, bottles, breast pump and supplies, Sophie the giraffe, sun hat, diapers, wipes, butt paste, baby shampoo, eczema cream, stroller—you get the idea—and headed out. She later told of how utterly miserable it was from the start. The second she boarded the flight, the baby had a blowout, which she then attempted to change in a baby-changing-station-less airplane bathroom. The changes in pressure greatly bothered baby's ears, and she screamed for the entire two-hour flight. Fellow passengers were not empathetic and shot her many disapproving glares. She and her husband were helpless. She cried.

You may have heard that vacations with littles are not vacations—they're trips. All the childcare that occurs at home continues. I'm sure there are many who feel a vacation with a baby is a nice change of scenery. Some little ones will peacefully sleep through an entire flight or a long car ride. Deciding to take baby on a trip or stay home is a personal choice and a roll of the dice.

Here's the take-home message: having a baby or toddler does not lend itself well to any semblance of the come-and-go-as-you-please life you enjoyed prior to having children. My friend wished she had waited on that vacation.

Adjusting to a beautiful baby takes time. You have now shifted from young professional to young parent. It's a new life stage. Please give yourself the room and space to adapt. And while you're at it, you must know: the days are long, but the years are short. Truly. The exhaustion will subside and transform into always evolving challenges and awesomeness. In the meantime, make the adjustments you feel are right for you.

Loving on Yourself

God created your irreplaceable soul for a very specific purpose, and being a mom is no minor part. You are critically important. You are now responsible for this precious little one who will one day go out and face this often tough, confusing world. And she will do it with excellence because she had you to show her the way. You are needed. You are so important to him and are so very needed. You are needed for the long haul. This means that a high level of love and care you provide to yourself just became mandatory.

There is an excellent reason that the concept of self-care has become permanently attached to motherhood. It's critical. You give so much of yourself to this beautiful new life that it's easy to have zilch left over. You will burn out if not intentional about self-care. Burnout leads to yelling. Burnout leads to relationship strain, a focus on the crazy over the cuddles, and an overall lousy string of weeks or months. You cannot be your best if you allow yourself to get to this place.

Self-care and daily "uplifters" can look many different ways. I'm going to throw some ideas at you here, but the key is to really think about a few things you loved to do before having your baby, and problem-solve until you can make that (or some version of it) a mainstay in your weekly routine.

Some moms like to splurge on really comfortable bedding to luxuriate unpredictable sleep that now includes middle-of-the-night feedings and morning cuddles. A really bright or inspirational coffee mug can be nice. A bath with delicious smelling salts, an on-demand stretch session on the floor with baby by your side, a walk with a fellow mom, or cheerful music playing at any time of day can be little uplifters. Besides the small things, look for some other substantial opportunities to love on yourself—and don't be afraid to ask for help.

Shutting Off Mom-mode

It is an absolute must for you to have time during the week when you can shut off mom-mode. Mom-mode is the turbo-charged mental state you are in when responsible for your child. You are unceasingly alert, aware, and anticipating. You're mentally tracking feedings, diaper changes, and shrinking inventory in both the pantry and diaper changing area. You notice the need for a nap before an overtired child emerges, and with infrared-like ability, can spot a choking hazard on the floor five seconds before your child puts it in his mouth. You plan for the trip out, and have all soothing, distraction-inducing, clean-up, and snack items on hand. This and much more all coincides with continuous supervision. You are "always on." I devote the entire next chapter to how to shift from Mr. and Mrs. to Mommy and Daddy. Lining up help beyond your husband is *strongly* advised in these early years to solidify regular breaks from mom-mode.

It's ironic, but in order to get a break from the work of motherhood you have to *do* some work! If you have trustworthy family members nearby who are willing to babysit—count that as a major blessing. If you don't, it will take time up front to integrate babysitting fees into the monthly budget, find and interview sound babysitters, and align schedules. It may be helpful to ask your friends with kids and similar values for babysitter recommendations. You will then need to inform the babysitter of your child's schedule, expectations, bedtime routines, and any other requirements you have. Once you get some regulars established, the time you put in will pay for itself hundreds of times over! If you do not secure regular help, you are leaving some joy on the table alongside patience, understanding, empathy, and teaching moments. You need regular time to love on yourself, fill your bucket, and recenter. Check out my "Deepening Your Babysitter Bench" bonus handout for other ideas on how to find great babysitters: lori-arnold.com/book.

If you don't think you need time off, I encourage you to try it anyway. You and your child will benefit if you keep your tank full, which is very hard to do if you never get to shut mom-mode down. You need time for you. Outside a paying job. Outside your marriage. Outside your baby. Just for you. Here are some ideas for more substantial self-care.

Exercise! Exercise is a remarkable self-care activity because not only does it provide tangible physical and mental benefits, but it can also lead to finding a community of friends. Alternatively, there are many great fifteen or twenty-minute exercise options of all varieties ready for you anytime, from your home, on demand. Exercise of any type or length of time makes us feel better and helps counteract many of the repetitive postures we assume as moms. Never has anyone regretted a workout.

If you enjoy feeling put together, perhaps an afternoon at a friend's house for some nail painting is something you can look forward to. In those early weeks, taking an uninterrupted nap may be just what you need. Maybe you could schedule an afternoon with a good book at a coffee shop. I have always found time dedicated to prayer brings a grounding perspective, increased gratitude, and a day in which things divinely work out better than when I allow God to slip to the back of my mind. Of course, there are tons of alternatives. The key is to *make it happen.*

Leave Comparison Behind

A final heads-up I'd like to give you in this area of embracing uncertainty relates to our human tendency to compare.

Confidence is built with experience. Unfortunately, we all start at ground zero with baby number one. As you work through the natural learning experience of early motherhood, please, please, please avoid a common pitfall: revisiting middle school.

The combination of new territory plus an off-the-charts desire to be a great mom can lead us to be overly attentive to what the "cool kids" are doing. In our isolated exhaustion, we may envy the (artificial) togetherness of other moms who appear relaxed, confident, trendy, and hauling an impressive social calendar. Or, we may feel like we're shortchanging our child if we don't emulate the mom whose kid's activity and development plan rival that of a pro athlete.

You may find yourself asking questions like these:

- Should I also enroll us in that mom-and-me class?

- Is my kid keeping up with his peers?

- Is my career going to suffer because I leave work earlier than my co-workers?

Don't do this! Find a few trusted friends or lean on your mom or sister or aunt. Talk with those who truly know you and share your values. Look to them and no one else. Reject comparison and gossip. Leave judgmental moms behind. Though you are a new mom, you have the most important experience already within you. You know your values. You know that cute clothes, bags, and shoes can be fun, but in the big picture they don't matter. Later on, I'll give you some tips on the activity and development front.

Please do not let insecurity lead to comparison or dampen your confidence. I cannot emphasize enough how entirely different kiddos are. I distinctly recall when a one-year-old in my daughter's playgroup counted to fifteen. My daughter couldn't even count to ten! Did I need to spend more time working with her on numbers? (For what it's worth, attempting organized learning at her young age was beyond frustrating and may have been an early math turnoff—not my desired outcome.) Later, the brainchild's mom said that she wasn't working with her son on counting. Her best guess was that he picked it up from *Sesame Street*.

All of us, including our children, have a unique set of gifts, interests, and abilities. Our job is to nurture the God-created interests and talents in our children, not push them toward premature milestone achievement.

Finally, know yourself. Pinterest is crawling with craft ideas for kids. I felt like I was robbing my children of their childhood by avoiding crafts—but I HATE crafts. Letting my kids play with playdough or sidewalk chalk or kinetic sand *outside* was just fine. I didn't need to let crafts suck the life out of me simply because all the other moms seemed to be craft wizards. As with any phase of life, judgment and comparison don't serve us. Create a filter tightly laced by your faith, values, and instincts, and use it to sift through those natural early motherhood uncertainties.

Let middle school comparison tendencies remain happily in the past. There is zero need to succumb to comparison—it only makes us feel inadequate.

Be Encouraged; Love Carries the Day

Be encouraged as you transition to the role of "Mom." While your priorities will shift, they do so for the greatest of all purposes: You are selfless. You sacrifice. You give more than you even know you have—all because you *love.*

Your child will feel every ounce of that love. You are providing him with irreplaceable comfort and security during these important months and years of his early life. There is a peace that comes when surrendering to the changes a baby brings. This time can be quite freeing as we recognize and focus our attention on that which is far greater than ourselves. Find little daily uplifters, line up outside help for more substantial self-love, and allow the sweetness, awe-inspiring growth, and love of your child to overtake the challenge of shifting priorities.

CHAPTER 2

Unpaid Champion Mom or Paid MVP Mom

I want to acknowledge straight away this might be an uncomfortable chapter. The topic of work among mothers continues to be a hot, contentious one. Our deep longing to give our kids the very best can result in superficial self-validation by way of defensiveness and judgment. Even today, our society tells us that "stay-at-home moms have it easy" and "working moms care more about their career than their kids." Both statements are nonsense.

If you find yourself getting defensive or comparative, know that these thoughts spring from a good place of wanting to do the best for yourself and your family. Then, recognize it does not serve you or anyone else and applaud all freshman moms for working our butts off—because we all do. Please shower love, not judgment, onto other moms. We need it.

My singular goal with this book is to give you information that will help you be the mom *you* want to be. Whether you plan to return to full-time employment, scale back your paid job, or transition to staying home with your child full-time, I believe it is important to give you a heads-up regarding various considerations that accompany these scenarios.

Whether you choose to return to some level of employment after maternity leave or care for your babe full-time, the shift in how you spend your time and the accompanying challenges are considerable. No matter how much you prepare, they're still bound to come as a surprise. Why? Because time is finite. For any new mom, demand far exceeds supply. The unachievable magic formula comes down to how you allocate this deficient resource. How many slices will you make in your personal pie of time and energy, how big or small will each slice be, and how will you manage them?

Trade-offs are unavoidable. Stay home with your kids and you get more of *everything*: More diapers, meltdowns, and messes. More cuddles, laughter, and spontaneous teaching moments. As it relates to mothering, returning to a paid job is the flip side. You will deal with fewer power struggles, nap-time battles, and cleanup—and you'll also experience fewer moments of cuddly goodness.

Of course, there are more detailed considerations to consider. If you are a single mom, the choice to maintain employment or not is not a choice at all. You have my prayers and sincerest admiration. You are the brightest of all rock stars. I also acknowledge that many families cannot make ends meet without two incomes. For others, it makes sense for Mom to provide for the family financially while Dad takes care of the baby. You will do what needs to be done. Moms always do.

For those blessed to have a choice regarding work, let me be obnoxiously clear: There is no right or wrong. Many variables come into play that can make or break a particular scenario. The demands of a job, husband involvement, personal temperaments, commute time, outside help, family goals, financial needs, child needs, and personal priorities must all be considered. The uniqueness of each one of us and our circumstances means the right choice for you or me might not be right at all for our neighbor. With that in mind, here's a heads-up on what to expect with regard to working, whether as a "paid MVP mom" (formerly known as a "working mom") or an "unpaid champion mom" (formerly known as a "stay-at-home mom").

First, Why the New Terms?

The historical terms for the work we do no longer cuts it. The term "working mom" is offensive to moms who have left paid employment because it implies they don't work. The term "full-time mom" can be offensive to employed moms because it implies they are only a mom part-time.

Literally speaking, the term "stay-at-home mom" (SAHM) is outdated and inaccurate, as more moms than ever before are earning a paycheck remotely while they—stay home. Additionally, the term "SAHM" continues to carry with it an inexperienced stereotype of ease. The truth is that when kids are young, all working scenarios are challenging. Any scenario for a mom with a young child is 24/7.

So, I'm leaving semantics behind and focusing on what matters—the career considerations you need to explore as you add a baby to the mix. First up: Transitioning to an unpaid champion mom.

Cons of Transitioning to Unpaid Champion Mom

There is decent amount of chatter in the news related to women and their accomplishments in the workforce. Women are (in the best possible way) encouraged to take up more seats at important tables. The unintended consequence of this public discourse is that the critical work of child-rearing is getting pushed toward insignificance.

Lack of Validation

Society does not view mothering as a career. Though you will polish many transferable skills, including time management, agility, problem solving, and many others, hiring professionals do not advise putting our mom-job on a resume. Rather, our society encourages champion moms to volunteer or find some activity to fill in a "resume gap" if we want to look for an outside job after taking time away to care for our children. I always pause when filling out the employment line on medical forms. Once, I just left it blank. The receptionist asked for an explanation. My part-time job was secondary at that point. My primary job was taking care of my child. So, I told her I was a mom. "So, you don't work?" she responded. This unintentionally degrading comment delivered the message that caring for my kids was not as important as a job that put money in the bank. This sums up the societal mentality many champion moms feel. It's essential that champion moms have an inner conviction about their world-changing work, despite living in a society where public-validation scales tip toward employment.

Adding to this are substantial changes that further challenge a champion mom's self-actualization. Champion moms may quickly shift from being financially independent, fulfilled, working women with daily interactions among like-minded professionals and mentors, to mostly isolated caregivers. New moms get little interaction, recognition, or any of the external validation provided by the paying job they held prebaby.

Before having kids, I had a job in business. It made me feel special. It challenged me. I was surrounded by wonderful colleagues and mentors. I was financially independent. I had hardware on my desk. I was gaining valuable experience in my chosen field to complement the education I had just spent years of my life attaining. And, in an instant, it was all gone. My ego wasn't ready for the shift.

Identity Shifts

To some degree, most of us view ourselves in light of our work. "What do you do?" is often the first question exchanged among new acquaintances. In transitioning to motherhood after beginning—and often advancing—a career, it can easily startle a new mom to not be able to identify with that role any longer. This is true even after a well-considered choice to take on the role of champion mom.

As you leave your financial independence behind, be aware of the potential for a changing money/power dynamic within the home, which may be real or perceived. Paying bills seems to always be the immediate priority before childcare and household needs. On the urgent and importance continuums, the paying job is always both urgent and important.

Unfortunately, child development and household management are often seen as somewhat important, and rarely urgent. Why does this matter? Your husband's assessment of his need to put in extra hours—whether late nights, weekends, or holidays—leaves you with little choice but to shoulder a full fourteen-hour day with your child whenever this assessment is made. Tension also arises when earning money is viewed as being more central than child-raising. This can result in feeling like your husband's time (including his downtime) takes precedence. If his role or time is seen as more important than yours, an unhealthy power imbalance emerges.

However, it's important to know that your work in managing the many aspects of child and household management is every bit as valuable as earning a paycheck. In fact, salary.com puts an annual value of over $180,000 on it! There is much more to cover when it comes to partnering with your husband, so stay tuned for that in the following chapters.

Feelings of Isolation

In addition to identity instability, unpaid champion moms often experience isolation and the need to connect. Never before in your life have you been alone for such an extended period of time. School, work, and extracurriculars had you surrounded by friends, peers, and other adult humans on a daily basis. Abruptly, these interactions are gone. Being with a baby or toddler all day does not meet our human need for connection. All socialization has to be planned and orchestrated around your new bundle of joy. In addition to being largely alone, the challenges of actual caretaking were greater than I anticipated as well (I didn't have a heads-up!).

Relentless Responsibilities

Not only was I missing the fulfillment and misplaced validation my prebaby job provided, but the struggle was amplified by the new responsibilities I was performing without end. I was now primarily feeding, cleaning, soothing, tracking, and worrying. Around six-to-nine-months, supervision intensified as naps shortened and baby's ability to move around increased. The combination of mobility without any concept of danger meant that my eyes and ears were on my child every minute she was awake. Nap time was spent on the adulting tasks of cleaning, meal-planning, home repairs, laundry, calling insurance about that incorrect bill, and completing dozens of other quietly needed tasks. It was relentless and exhausting. I was clocking nearly seventeen thousand steps a day with zero effort.

My saneness fled quickly at any sustained amount of crying. Children know how to do one thing when they aren't happy—cry (which later, gives way to whining). It takes a long time to teach this out of them. Dealing with it in the meantime zapped my patience on more occasions than I'd like to admit. At one point or another, champion moms want to walk off the job.

The days I worked an outside job part-time served as a break of sorts. Yet, it also added a layer of stress and responsibility as I worked to provide excellent service to my clients, kept up with pumping, and orchestrated everything the babysitter needed while I was away.

Pros of Transitioning to Unpaid Champion Mom

Now, it's certainly not all bleak. There is an abundance of awesome that far outweighs the hard when it comes to the champion mom path.

Going from Two Jobs to One

While I hope your prebaby job provided you with fulfillment, we all know that outside jobs can be stressful. There are deadlines, fire drills, bad managers, rude customers, and a host of performance metrics to meet. Cell phones and the internet have made it all the more difficult to truly be "off" when it's time to shift your attention to your child. Becoming a champion mom takes these burdens off the table. While moms of littles are constantly on the move, they can complete many tasks without a deadline nearing or an inbox piling up. I think about moms who have paid employment as having two jobs. Transitioning away from an outside career allows champion moms to focus on just one.

As a mostly unpaid champion mom, I've thought many times about how grateful I am to have time to do the job. I'm thankful I don't have to cut my sleep down to six hours if I want to get a workout in. I love having the time, and patience, to sit and read with my kids each night, research child development and discipline techniques, find and test meals they might actually eat, and show them how to make granola bars. I appreciate having the time to calculate and prepare my daughter's medically prescribed meals. I'm so thankful I don't have to do all the adulting—get the car repaired, file the taxes, update the kids' closets, or research if I really can save 15% on my insurance—on the fringes of weekdays or on weekends. I'm grateful that our family doesn't surpass our stress maximum when a snow day, illness, or critical home repair hits. I'm so thankful that I don't have to stay up until eleven at night or use vacation days to stuff Easter eggs, wrap Christmas gifts, or plan birthday celebrations. As an uptight, type-A mom, managing many of life's tasks while the sun is up allows me to be more relaxed and joyful with my children. I again sit in awe of single moms.

Patience

Another major advantage to becoming a champion mom, especially for my get-it-done personality, was patience. Oh my word, do you need a monumental amount of patience in order to parent with a teaching mindset versus a "Stop now!" one.

Certainly, my patience had often left the building by the end of a day's worth of fussing, messes, and orchestration. However, I found I could handle the vast amount of crying, whining, endless requests, irrationality, and messes with far more patience (and thus effectiveness) than if these things were being tacked onto the stress I'd historically brought home from an outside job. This meant that my kids spent most of their time with smiling, silly, teacher Mommy during the day before "over-it" Mom remained clocked in for the evening shift.

Humility

No two mothering journeys are the same, but for me, an unexpected blessing of stepping away from my career was a kick in the rump. As you might have gathered, I had allowed my previous job to provide me with validation. Hard as we try, most of us attach some level of our identity (and even worth) to our career. I went from being a pretty big fish in a small pond to an ocean filled with same-sized fish. Now there was nothing setting me apart. No awards. No respectable salary. No management title.

God was working on me here. He used this phase of motherhood to build in me the greatest of all virtues: Humility. It was in this place I really began to see other people. I began to recognize the massive value people, with unique backgrounds and experiences, were making to our world in a million different ways. An impressive job does not make us special. God does. I hadn't fully internalized that.

Being There for It All

Perhaps the greatest of all blessings of becoming a champion mom is the sheer fact that you get to be there for it *all*.

No one loves your baby more than you. As a champion mom, you get to shower that love onto your child all day long. You can kiss his cheeks endlessly. You get to witness every awe-inspiring milestone. You can nurse far more easily and enjoy the irreplaceable moments of your baby sleeping on your chest. You get to take in every smile, every laugh, and each new discovery.

Instilling Values and Life-Affecting Lessons

As your baby grows, you get to take advantage of the endless spontaneous teaching moments that arise each day. Being with your children throughout the day presents you with many opportunities to talk about your values, offer early opportunities to grow their independence, and instill important lessons.

I cannot downplay how early kids learn life-affecting lessons and mindsets. My heart absolutely melted when my two-year-old daughter, unprompted, picked up some trash while walking together along our typical neighborhood route. When an opportunity arose to showcase caring about others, I took it. I told her what I was doing when I closed a neighbor's mailbox or when I picked up trash that didn't belong to me. We prayed in the middle of the day to thank God for the sunshine. We asked Him to watch over the first responders and the person they were on their way to help when we heard sirens. Being present at the park allowed me to witness her behavior with others, and thus recognize the need to talk to her about being a leader others want to follow. Being at my daughter's gymnastics class allowed me cheer her on and boost her pride each time she yelled, "Mom, watch this!"

Tips for the New Champion Mom

While there were many, many days I wished I was back in my cubicle, I have no regrets. If you are considering a shift to champion mom, I would like to offer a few tips.

Wait on the Side Hustle

Please give yourself grace on the side hustle. Our education and professional experience often (prematurely) leads us to jump into some sort of outside endeavor. Many of us deal with an invisible force that makes us feel like we should do more. I tried to start a blog, then pulled back when I became increasingly discouraged at the lack of uninterrupted time I could dedicate. I'll never forget the time I was trying to write while my one-year-old had crawled to my desk and was screaming at my feet. I let her scream while I tried to finish my thought. That was the last time I did that. Being a mom of little kids consumes everything. They are not yet capable of being independent for any measurable amount of time. I promise you can get that side hustle going in years to come.

A Need to Plan

Some champion moms do plan to re-enter the workforce down the line. If this is a goal of yours, make a plan.

If you are interested in becoming a paid MVP mom after some time home with your child, lay out your ideal timing and ideal work. Do you want to go back to the type of work or employer that you had prebaby? Are you interested in a job that allows more flexibility than your previous job offered?

Having a general idea of your longer-term goals will allow you to avoid the limbo many champion moms find themselves in. You will enjoy your time with your kids more. It will also help you focus on the small steps you can take in the interim to set yourself up for success. Maybe you'd like to slowly pick up outside work by getting involved in the ever-growing "gig" economy.

If you have future workforce aspirations, I encourage you to keep up with networking by sending messages and commenting on posts via LinkedIn. As you think about your longer-term plans, recognize they can always shift. I was warned about and can attest to the fact that while daytime hours *do* open up when the youngest child starts attending a preschool or kindergarten, there remains a ton of school breaks, sick days, e-days, parent-teacher conference days, and the like. After-school activities increase as well. Whatever you do, never forget to give yourself grace through these major considerations.

Cons of Transitioning to Paid MVP Mom

In many ways, transitioning to being a paid MVP mom is the flip side of the champion mom coin. I'll start with the challenges.

You Now Have Two Jobs

Rather than transitioning from a full-time job to full-time caregiving, employed moms maintain an outside job, facilitate childcare while they're at work, and add to their plate the many aspects of child-raising during the hours when they are not earning a paycheck.

While moms returning to an outside job may not experience the identity challenges many champion moms experience, leaving a young child for a large part of the day has potential to bring about different feelings of inadequacy, guilt, and stress.

Moms who return to employment now literally have two jobs. Outside jobs have already stretched the limits of time as organizations have been pushing for decades to do more with less. You will be "on" from the moment you wake up and get yourself and your kids ready for the day, until you get into bed after a day packed with your outside job followed by the weekly laundry, grocery shopping, meal prep, cleaning, facilitating home repairs, and tending to the physical, mental, and emotional needs of your child. Handling the unanticipated sick days; arranging for standard pediatrician appointments; and playing the role of birthday-party planner, St. Nicholas, and Easter Bunny lay the very foundation for the cliché that there is "not enough time in a day." This paves the way for weight MVP mothers often carry: guilt.

"Mom and guilt might as well be the same word."

—Patty

Mom Guilt

Your organization, your husband, and your kids need you. There often isn't enough of you to go around, which can lead to a feeling of failing. It must have been an MVP mom who coined the phrase, "You can't be all things to all people."

My heart broke for a colleague of mine who could not manage to hold back her tears in those first few days back after maternity leave. She did adjust to her new norm, as will any MVP mom who faces the incredibly difficult moment of leaving her baby and heading back to the figurative (or perhaps literal) office. Guilt can also creep in if you miss a milestone like baby's first words, steps, or newfound belly laugh.

There will be times when your paying job requires the majority of your energy and times when your mom job will need it. It can be especially hard when you just are not able to spend the time with your child that you would like.

A friend I used to work with sent out a heart breaking plea to her network, asking how they keep track of everything. She had missed an event at her child's daycare and felt just terrible about it.

A side note on the guilt: Many well-intentioned mom-cheerleaders will tell you to eliminate guilt. "It doesn't serve you," they say. If you can do this, bravo to you. I think guilt is a natural consequence of taking on so many things of such great importance. It's also a clue that something might be off. Our feelings often contain important insights. Maybe an adjustment needs to be made. Maybe you've had more than a few weeks of intense work and your gut is telling you some dedicated kid-time is in order. If you find yourself feeling guilty, stop, consider it, and then move ahead with your intentional, well-considered choice. I'll talk more about choices and intentions later.

Spread Too Thin

I cannot overstate the challenge new MVP moms endure due to being spread so thin. Notice I have not yet said anything about time for—drumroll please—yourself! "Me time" becomes a distant memory as the fixed number of hours in a day are spent being both a great employee and a great mom. Many MVP moms feel guilty about spending any of their limited time outside of work doing something for themselves. They are already away from their kiddo for hours each day and want to be there the rest of the time. Those working moms who prioritize important "me time" often sacrifice significant sleep. (You might be thinking, *What about Dad?* As promised, I offer more on the critical parenting partnership coming up.)

Stress on Stress

Know that patience is one of the greatest things our kids need from us. Providing this patience becomes harder when you bring home the stresses of an unreasonable boss, the emotional toll of rude customers, or the anxiety of unfinished tasks from an outside job. As I hope to effectively communicate throughout this book, children are stressful (awesome, but stressful). Some days, stress is piled on top of stress. Even after the most challenging days, you still must come home and care for your kids, who may or may not have had a good day themselves. Morning routines of getting dressed, fed, and out the door on time can be hard. The outside job can be hard. Your kids might also have a hard day with interrupted naps, teething pain, and the like. The evening may then be filled with frustration, yelling, and tears over standard child-development mishaps. There may be stretches of time where it feels like you aren't getting much bucket-filling time with your young child.

Fewer Organic Teaching Moments

Working an outside job naturally results in fewer opportunities to take advantage of spontaneous teaching moments. I'm not talking about teaching ABCs, but the character-building life lessons and family values not taught in any daycare or classroom.

Do not fear. As long as your child knows they are your number-one priority, they will be fine. A plethora of successful, well-adjusted, morally strong kids showcase firsthand that this is not a deal-breaker. It's just another aspect to recognize and proactively manage as you carve your own motherhood path. You will have to work with greater intention to instill your family values into your child.

Pros of Transitioning to Paid MVP Mom

Now, let's shift to the many benefits of being an MVP mom after baby.

Financial

Obviously, a huge pro of becoming a paid MVP mom is the financial aspect. You have more money in the bank, assuming you earn more than the cost of childcare. You also have financial independence and a security blanket in case you or your husband lose a job. Your resume will remain shiny and current with ever-growing experience. You also will have no concern about how to get back into the workforce after time away. You never left.

Professional Fulfillment and Adult Interaction

You will continue to receive any fulfillment that your outside job provides. You will continue to learn from managers, colleagues, customers, and mentors. Your outside job will provide you with daily opportunities to interact with other adults, thus isolation will be a nonissue.

Chipping Away at Glass Ceilings

A wonderful benefit of being an MVP mom is the one you provide to people like me. MVP moms set examples and establish opportunities for all girls and women. A strong showing of women in the workforce coupled with my education and experience is empowering. I know I can get a full-time paid job if I need to.

Better yet, my daughters will grow up knowing that they are bound only by their own thinking. They have choice. There is no predetermined destiny dictating that they must be a homemaker or childcare provider or remain in a toxic relationship for financial reasons. We all have this because women everywhere are rocking it at jobs across all levels in every industry. If it were not for an army of inspirational MVP moms, I would feel suppressed and discouraged about the lack of opportunities for myself and my girls.

As if that weren't enough, I am eternally grateful for all the moms who serve my family directly. My daughter's neurologist, dietician, pediatrician, therapists, tutors, and teachers are moms, and many have youngsters. Most of my healthcare providers are moms. My awesome Starbucks barista, the patient flight attendant, the understanding grocery store clerk, and countless others are adding such value to my family and our communities on the whole.

Structured Adult-Sanity Time

While this does not hold for all, I have had more than a few MVP moms tell me their employment provides a "break" of sorts. I even heard a mom of toddlers say: "I wouldn't even survive if I was not working." Little children regularly test the limits of adult sanity. There is a completely different and unending mental realm that we operate in when caring for our children's basic needs, teaching them literally everything (no, we cannot use our toy hammer on the window), fielding "mom" requests hundreds of times a day, and remaining on high safety alert. MVP moms get a chance to turn this part of their brain off. You can get a cup of coffee or chat with a co-worker without having to drop everything at the sound of a crash, someone yelling "Mom!," or silence—which could mean your child is smearing poop on the walls. You can enjoy a kind of peace that doesn't exist in a home with littles. This childcare break can also lead to feeling like a better mom.

An MVP friend of mine talked about how excited she was to pick up her child every day. She felt very fulfilled in her work, appreciated the social interaction her child was getting at daycare, and came home each evening full of enthusiasm to spend time with her child. For her, it's about quality of time over quantity. Of course, some MVPs have the opposite evening experience. It is all very individual. There will be good and bad days regardless of your job choice.

Creating Your Community

For all moms, the greatest factor that will influence your happiness and your ability to be the mom you want to be is your bench.

Consider the following questions: What kind of help, if any, are you going to have? Do you have grandparents nearby who are willing to watch your child? How demanding is your outside job, if you maintain one? How flexible is it? What does your husband's job require? What needs does your child have? What help will you have during evenings and weekends, when a call comes in to pick up your sick child, or a snow day shuts down daycare?

MVP moms in particular will find comfort by putting in the up-front work to establish solid childcare, since this person or business will be spending a significant amount of time with your child. Sometimes, it may seem like you don't have much choice and must use whatever help you can find. Do not accept it. Interview care providers and set expectations, especially as you get into the toddler years. As previously mentioned, teaching moments happen all day long. Those little eyes and ears are taking in *every* situation. Do you want your care provider to reinforce independent behavior? Do you want them to praise your child's effort versus their intelligence? (Research says yes.) Do you want them to pray before meals? Do you want them to work on any academics like letter sounds? The more up-front work now, the more peace of mind you will have when you are away.

For champion and MVP moms alike, the level and quality of help you have (or don't) can completely alter your early mothering experience. Be aware that some childcare facilities have wait-lists of a year or longer, so get started early. Set yourself up for success with a strong bench of helpers.

Think Outside the Career Box

If you're thinking to yourself, *There are so many cons, no matter the path,* fear not. I've read that the happiest new moms work outside the home—part-time.

Be bold! If you're interested, research opportunities to scale back your outside job, increase job flexibility, or shift into a role or organization known for its support of moms. If nothing seemingly exists, put on your problem-solving hat. Think of ways you could meet the needs of your employer, gain the help you need at home, and critically, be your happiest during this wonderfully challenging phase of life. Talk with your manager or a trusted mentor. You'll never uncover a potential win-win unless you light the fire.

Of course, like anything else, there are two sides to the part-time coin. Some feel a split focus results in them not doing any one thing particularly well. Again, all employment/mom scenarios are very individual.

No matter your career path, where it leads, or how you choose to trek it, know that you have far more control than it may seem. Things take time and experience. You can always pivot. Life is one big learning process and motherhood accelerates it tenfold. You may not truly understand the ins and outs of your job choice or the new challenges that will arise until you live it. No worries. This isn't a one-shot deal.

If you head back to work and realize that too little irreplaceable time with your child is available, you can step away. If you care for your kids as a champion mom and feel you aren't fulfilled or would be a better mom if you had an outside job, you can pursue that.

No matter our situation, we can always do the work, make the change, and go after the life we envision. As you find your way, remember to check in with yourself: Are you happy? What is working? What isn't? Is God trying to tell you anything? Never be afraid to make changes in the direction of your instincts.

Looking back, it's pretty incredible how God used early motherhood to make me a better person. It was never in my grand plan to leave my career. Ever. God led me to this place and used it to move me in ways I needed to be moved. I used to think life changed my plans. Now I realize God changed my plans because he loves me and guides me. He will do the same for you. Stay in prayer. Our Creator uses motherhood to build and strengthen us in countless, often hidden, ways. Let that sink in on the hard days.

Invest in What Truly Matters to You

I'd like to leave one final thought for anyone whose heart is pulling them home, but their bank account is pulling them away. If your job is about money rather than personal fulfillment, I encourage you to spend some time with pen and paper.

Many cultural forces surround us (most fueled by marketers and influencers) that lead us to believe we need a lot of stuff. And it needs to be high-end: Sweet clothes, a two-story brick house with a pool, organic food, the newest gaming system, *all* the streaming services, the cutest baby clothes, chic coffee, the expensive baby bouncer, the trendsetting sunglasses, an admirable SUV... and on and on.

We don't actually need this stuff. We just don't. Sure, life is expensive when you consider things like healthcare, college savings, and diapers. It may very well be the case that you *do* need to have an outside job to secure the basic needs of your family.

However, do your work on this: If you really, *really* want to be home with your babies, but think you cannot afford to, pull out your budget.

Understand any insurance or benefits that will change if you step away. Factor in the cost of childcare, which is not cheap! Look at your spending and put that red pen to work. It may be possible to trade in a few steaks, early-adopter status on clothing and tech trends, and an extra bedroom for more time with your little one. There are so many great sites like thredUP for trendy clothes, social media can help you find gently used baby everything, and at-home coffee is ready in minutes. I have found some name-brand kids' clothes with tags for mere dollars at the Goodwill in a nice, nearby suburb. Try living on a single income for a few months and see if you can make it work. You just might have more choices than you think.

As you navigate the challenges of a career, please hear me say, *It's all going to be OK.* You *are* a great mom. Otherwise, you wouldn't be investing in yourself and this book. And here's the best news: There is no wrong answer. I take that back—the only wrong answer is if you follow someone else's path versus forging your own.

The Power of Prayer

If you are uncertain about the future of your postbaby career, I encourage you to pray on it. It's always a good idea to take our questions and uncertainties to the Lord and ask for His guidance. Not only were you fearfully and wonderfully made, but God has a unique purpose for your life. Never stop working to align your life with this divine purpose, as this is where the greatest joy awaits. No matter your job choice, there will be pros and cons, give and take. You can focus on what you've lost, or you can focus on what you've gained. Focus on the gain. Adjust where needed.

Whatever your chosen path, I encourage you to detach your identity from your job. You are so much more. You are more than a teacher or marketer or nurse or cashier or saleswoman or retail specialist—or mom. Our value is not based on the positions we've held, the accolades we've received, the money we've earned, or how many children we have. We are a unique set of God-given talents, abilities, and experiences through which we make the world better. You will always be more than your job, whether it pays or not. You are invaluable. Never forget it.

CHAPTER 3

From Mr. and Mrs. to Mommy and Daddy

Bringing a baby into the world is one of the most magnificent, life-changing experiences a couple can share. It's almost too magical to comprehend. You and your husband share the greatest of all blessings, and along with it, the desire to raise a strong, confident, happy, God-loving child. Both of your priorities shift to ensure this precious baby is taken care of. It's the ultimate in "being in it together."

Co-parenting requires the greatest of all partnerships. Now that the demands on your time and energy have increased exponentially, it is infinitely important to work through, *in microscopic detail*, how you and your husband will be partner parents. There is a great myth floating about that a baby strengthens a relationship. The opposite is true. Counselor Molly Millwood, PhD, notes that having a baby is actually a risk factor for divorce. She also notes that new parents argue nine times more than they did during their prebaby days. These are hard facts to read, but internalizing them will allow you to get ahead of the forces that lead to these statistics and write a different story for your family. Let's start by talking about some challenges to look out for due to the sheer fact that God created men and women very differently.

The Noticer and the Nothing Box

God reserved some pretty amazing gifts for us women.

Women notice. Usually *everything*. We see what needs to be done and knock it out—cleaning, fixing, food expiration, payment deadlines, when the towels need washing and the sheets need changing, etc. The number of things needing to be noticed has now increased a hundred times over. As international marriage speaker Mark Gungor noted in his YouTube talk "A Tale of Two Brains," we women have completely connected brains. Our husbands' brains, on the other hand, have a bunch of independent boxes that don't touch. In other words, they think differently. They tend to focus on more singular bits of information at a time. You can simultaneously change out the laundry, have dinner on the stove, talk to the pediatrician about your baby's rash, and notice his diaper is full. Your husband, on the other hand, likely won't showcase this ability.

Gungor also notes that men prefer to spend as much time as possible in their "nothing" box. They need time to think about nothing or to not think at all. This can mimic the appearance of a "couch potato" or spark a need for your husband to escape to a "man cave." It can look like gaming, late-night TV watching, or any number of things that may appear unproductive to us moms. My husband talks often about needing a "break."

Beware of Resentment

Being the noticer with an interconnected brain while our husband regularly visits his nothing box often results in moms taking on more of the "unfun, just needs done" part of childcare. While many husbands are beginning to take on childcare tasks that were foreign to their fathers, moms still disproportionally carry the majority of the physical, and especially mental, load. This is a well-paved road to resentment I am far too familiar with.

A while back, my family of three was out for a rare, Saturday afternoon lunch. Our twelve-month-old daughter was sitting at the table in a high chair. After the waitress brought our side salads and drinks, my husband immediately dug in. He was oblivious to the fact that his sugary drink had been placed within reach of our child, nor did it occur to him that perhaps he should be the one keeping watch over her during this time. After all, I was the one up early with her while he had slept in that morning.

Now, I was not traveling on the high road at this particular time. Though I clearly anticipated what was about to happen, I decided (without a mature, adult conversation with him, of course) that it was my turn to give my brain a baby break. I sat back and watched my daughter knock over that full glass of soda, stickying up everything in it's wake. He and I then proceeded to have a very public blowup with no regard for our fellow restaurant-goers. I held nothing back in pointing out his selfishness and raged about how I shouldn't be expected to supervise our child around the clock. He tried to piecemeal an argument together that it was somehow *my* responsibility to move *his* drink.

While I would love to say that this embarrassing episode was a growth opportunity for us, we did not capitalize on it at the time. We continued similar meal time arguments every time I brought to his attention that perhaps *he* should take a turn cutting our daughter's food into tiny 'non-chokable' pieces before helping himself.

This is just one scenario I use to demonstrate a very common "who's in charge" conflict that arises when welcoming a baby. One of you must be the lead supervisor every second your child is not being watched by a third party. Every. Single. Second.

Appreciating the differences in how I operate versus my husband is an area I continue to work on in my own personal growth journey. I didn't recognize or appreciate my husband's need for time in his "nothing box." In my view, I was working around the clock, so he should be too. Why did he get to nap for three hours every Sunday afternoon when that kind of free time was nonexistent in my world? We both needed to do a better job of working together in adapting to our new normal.

These types of situations highlight that marriage is work. It takes work to address conflicts and team up to ensure resentment does not creep into your relationship. Praise the Lord for forgiveness and opportunities to try again. I continue to work toward getting on that high road through productive conversations versus arguments or passive-aggressive gestures. Here's another heads-up: This high road can be harder to travel when it comes to little, perpetual annoyances.

Understanding the Compound Effect

The increased workload that accompanies baby can magnify the already existing irritations you have with your husband.

Perhaps you never make a big deal about him leaving his dirty dishes in the sink. Maybe picking up his smelly socks from the living room is something you playfully bring to his attention. Perhaps you simply turn off the lights and properly seal up the box of crackers on his behalf.

When a baby arrives, this grace fades. Your tolerance for picking up after a grown man plummets in the face of the clean up you are now tackling on behalf of a baby who cannot do it for herself. These changes in your perspective, while seemingly little, are extremely important to recognize and stay on top of. Why? Because the compound effect is at play. It's the repetitious childcare, plus the lack of the sleep, plus the continued reminders to our husbands that blow our fuse. If you find yourself frequently short-circuiting, that's a sign you need more help and more self-care. Do not ignore it. Nothing is more important than the integrity of the family unit.

Adjusting to Changing Times and Changing Roles

Our society is in a unique place regarding traditional gender roles. Men on the whole have come a long way in their contributions beyond breadwinning. However, this progress is not felt equally by all wives. As more women desire to take their skills and ambition beyond childcare and domestic management, whether in the workplace or any number of endeavors, men's adjustment to this shift varies drastically from family to family. Some men are early adopters and see the need for equitable sharing of child and homecare responsibilities. Others are laggards. Where your husband falls on this scale will have a significant impact on how you now partner as parents.

In addition, the time needed to adjust to a new baby often varies between moms and dads. Most women will admit that their baby changed their life significantly more than it changed their husband's, at least initially. This can add additional fuel to the resentment fire. Welcoming my precious baby girl gave my life an automatic system update that put her care center stage. My loving husband's system update had some glitches and a time delay.

He was used to his prebaby, carefree weekends of sleeping in, enjoying some coffee while watching *SportsCenter*, and then hitting the gym. Meanwhile, I innately understood that my weekend mornings now began when the baby awoke, my gym time was in flux, and my weekends were just as full as my weekdays. We argued often about the specific window of time when he would be in charge of the baby. It took him longer to internalize that a baby requires a schedule, everyone is now working harder, and time off needed to be evenly distributed.

Meanwhile, I was becoming increasingly frustrated each time I witnessed a dad pushing a stroller on a Saturday morning or a group of new moms out for a stroller-free run. So, how do you change things if this imbalanced dynamic presents itself in your relationship? Here are some ways to help narrow the adjustment gap, regardless of how progressive or conservative your husband is when it comes to sharing in the domestic workload.

Ways to Adjust and Begin to Thrive

The first step you need to take is to recognize your husband's attitude toward childcare and household work. Where does he fall on the adjustment spectrum? This will inform how easily and quickly, or not, you can come up with a system that feels equitable to you both. Here are some strategies to help him adapt a little more easily (and quickly) to his new parenting reality:

- **Keep hubby's perception in check, if needed.** Some men have the misinformed notion that being home with a baby is easy-peasy. My husband would often tell me how "hard" his job was and lament that the weekends were his only time to recuperate. To me, this sounded like he was saying that my work from sunup to sundown each day, not to mention nighttime feedings, was not so tough and therefore didn't require the same recoup time. It's hard to understand the unending challenges of taking care of a young child unless you've done it. So, he needs to do it! Putting hubby on point of your baby's care will also help with critical early bonding.

"I was an overly generous wife and tried to do it all myself. I remember trying to take care of the baby on my own to let him (my husband) sleep. So, so silly of me."

—Katie

- **Don't assume hubby and baby have bonded.** Even if your husband appreciates the challenges involved in round-the-clock caregiving, men still naturally take longer to bond with baby. We had a nine-month head start and are wired to nurture. To help him catch up, in the earliest days, leave the baby alone with your husband on a regular basis. Go get your hair done. Visit a friend. Go to a coffee shop. Run errands. Go for a drive or find a friend's spare bedroom to nap in. If you are like me, this will not be something you want to do. Do it anyway, even if it is for short bouts of time. Your husband and child need time together to bond. The earlier, the better.

- **Work to grow his confidence with baby.** As your husband spends more time in charge of baby (without you being within reach to be the fixer of any issues), he will grow in his confidence and ability to take care of your precious bundle. He will also grow in appreciation of how difficult the caretaking role is as he experiences firsthand the vast number of feedings, diaper changes, bouts of crying, quantity of spit-up, and the like.

If you are exclusively breastfeeding, no problem. You can loosely schedule your time away directly after a feeding. This is a win-win: Your husband's confidence increases and your baby bonds with your husband, thus you aren't the one and only person capable of soothing a crying baby. And, you get essential time for yourself, which is critical to feeling like you haven't lost all agency in your life.

The alternative is a terrible feeling many new moms deal with: Having to *ask* our husbands for permission to make a hair appointment, go to the gym, or do anything solo. Without regularly scheduled times that Dad is in charge, you must secure his help or a sitter to do *anything* without baby in tow. Let me tell you, this dynamic breeds a constant undertone of discontentment.

In addition to carving out regular Daddy-baby time, communication is the foundation to a thriving family unit. Detailed, ongoing communication is a must. I'm talking weekly. Without it, a marriage can slowly erode over time.

"What if I told you your dad knows how to pour milk too?"

—Mom meme

- **Be a leader** for your family. At first, I held onto the poisonous notion that I shouldn't *have* to be the one in charge of everything, the one who notices everything. I shouldn't *have* to ask him to take on his fair share of parenting responsibilities. I shouldn't *have* to be the one to initiate conversations to work through issues. The truth is that I was forgetting one of the best pieces of advice I have ever received: Do I want to be right or do I want to be effective?

  Whether I should have to ask for my husband's help or lock in his parental supervision time is irrelevant. The bottom line is that I made my life dramatically more miserable by living in stubbornness. I refused to recognize the blessing of my integrated brain and the wonderfully nurturing qualities God reserved especially for moms. Knowing and anticipating childcare needs is something most of us moms rock at. I always felt this dynamic was unfair. But I know that life isn't fair and I have no business questioning my Creator. My husband has many strengths in other areas and is open to helping if I can get out of my own way long enough to ask for it.

- **Avoid nonproductive conflict** and grow together. God designed marriage for sanctification. Husbands and wives are to help each other grow closer to Him through this incredible vocation. It's a majorly awesome, majorly high calling.

Like all things, awesome tasks require effort. This effort grows in size and significance when the family is expanded. The challenges you and your spouse face together make up a sizeable piece of the overall growth process in our lives, and is only eased with grace, a proactive seeking of goodness in the other, appreciation, and a loving communication of needs. Productive conflict is good. Plain old conflict without the end game of win-win solutions rips a partnership apart one thread at a time.

Once resentment has set in, appreciation for one another has been lost, and openness to your partner's feedback is closed, the marriage is in a very dangerous place. *Get ahead of it.* Schedule regular husband-and-wife team meetings in the "neutral zone," where calm openness resides and heated emotions have subsided. Frustration never sparks productive conversation.

I am going to beg you for a moment: Please take this to the deepest part of your heart. When working through (or avoiding) critical co-parenting issues—or any marital issue for that matter—you can be like me and require time, repetitive arguments, and deep pain to show you that grace is the better path. Or you can heed my advice: Wait to address grievances until you can meet your teammate in the "neutral zone." Here, arguments become *productive* conflict. Of course, arguments are unavoidable in a relationship. We all flip out every now and again. But work through as many issues as possible in the neutral zone. If you find yourself having more bottles of wine than proactive check-ins with your husband, there is a problem.

- **Don't hesitate to seek counseling.** If you have tried to adjust things with your partner but your marriage is still suffering, try counseling! A contentious marriage, an unhappy partner, or the drips of resentment will not only weigh you down, they will negatively impact your child as well. Drop your ego here. Get help if its needed. As you institute regular check-ins, a topic that may need to be added to the agenda is sex.

- **Expect changes in the bedroom.** Many moms find their desire for bedroom time ceases, and remains low for some time, after giving birth. Your boobs have become feeding vessels. Even when the doctor gives you the thumbs up, your body isn't the same. You're tired.

My need for closeness and connection was more than being met by my baby. My desire for sex was nonexistent. Whether you're home with a child all day long or following up a day job with your mom job, it's all exhausting. Know that your husband's desire for sex will likely remain unaltered after baby comes.

I am far from alone when I admit that having one more human (my husband) need something from me (sex) at the end of the day was the absolute *last* thing I wanted to deal with. So, I'll say it again: get ahead of it. I can attest that the household will never exude a positive vibe when one partner is sexually frustrated. Yet, I do not advocate for submitting to unwanted intimate time in favor of keeping the peace. "Pushing the pain" often results in amplifying the pain, especially if you already feel you are carrying more than your fair share of the load. If you are not interested, it signals that you have needs that are every bit as important as his, that are not being met. Talk about it directly. Talk about it as often as needed. Talk about it in the neutral zone, not when he's already started the "I-want-to-have-sex-tonight" canoodling.

What should you do if sex is not a desired activity you want to add to the weekly calendar? Talk to your husband about what he can do to step up for you as he is asking you to step up for him. What can he take on so that you aren't as cashed at the end of the day? If the forty-five-minute, three-drinks, five-hugs, seven-kisses, I-have-to-go-potty, one-more-story, tell-me-about-your-day bedtime routine gets you good and ready for lights out yourself, perhaps your husband handles this. Are dinner, bathtime, and end-of-day cleanup sucking the last bit of life right out of you? Perhaps some of these responsibilities can move to his column. Many couples find they are much happier finding daytime opportunities (i.e., nap time) for intimacy. A misaligned interest in sex after baby arrives affects many couples. Proactively manage it in a way that works for both of you.

What's Best for You Is Best for Your Family Too

I hope your husband is an early adopter when to comes to the major adjustments that need made when expanding the family. If he's not, I encourage you to, with grace and kindness, relentlessly advocate for what you need.

Do not let your husband, advertently or inadvertently, make you feel that any time at home with your child, your career, or your personal ambition, is in any way less hard or less important than his. It is not. Period. You need time for yourself, just like he does. The childcare and household workload, the financial needs of the family, and the personal goals of you and your husband all need to be accounted for in the family plan. All major family decisions should be evaluated in light of what is best for the family unit.

What will enable you and your husband to thrive, both individually and within your marriage? What do your children need to thrive and come to know the love of Christ? Decisions spanning career, schooling, faith, lifestyle, geographical location, and other issues will have a significant impact on your family and need to be worked through. A huge part of the new family plan that will need to be worked through is the division of labor. This is covered in detail in the next chapter. Before we get there, I want to close this chapter by encouraging you to offer your husband grace through this major life transition.

Never forget, your husband loves you deeply. He loves your child deeply. In all likelihood, he is beyond amazed that you gave birth (or remained steadfast through a grueling adoption process). He likely stands in awe watching you provide your child with unrelenting love and care. He also doesn't have the benefit of the immediate bond you have with your child. While it's tough to be the one who primarily notices baby's needs or who can stop the crying, it's pretty wonderful to be the main target for all the cuddles, smiles, and love.

Our husbands simply need a little more time to bond and adjust. Try your best to give him that time, imbalanced as it may seem at times. God made us different on purpose. If we can keep the lines of communication open, institute Daddy-baby bonding time, and maintain gratitude that we have an awesomely integrated brain, we can better enjoy the true blessing that children are. I pray your child strengthens the partnership you have with your husband.

There is also one more substantial, often overlooked factor to consider if you feel your annoyance building: God blessed us with mom skills. We are inherently created to nurture. It's a gift, albeit one that I was regrettably bitter about for a time. I wanted my husband to have as much of this asset as I did. I wanted him to wake up at each baby whimper too.

But God has a different way and, as we all know, His ways are perfect. I encourage you to embrace this God-given gift while also helping your husband transition toward being an equal partner in your family's new normal.

Now that we have a handle on how a new baby can affect moms and dads differently, let's go deep into a life-changing topic that must be addressed when shifting from Mr. and Mrs. to Mommy and Daddy: The division of labor.

Has this book been helpful thus far?
If so, please consider helping other moms
find this resource by leaving a review
on your favorite online book retailer.
It means more than you know.

CHAPTER 4

It's a Team Effort

When you first got married, hopefully you and your husband developed a fair system for sharing the tasks of meal planning, cooking, cleaning, doing laundry, managing finances, paying bills, social planning, managing household goods inventory like soap and toilet paper, buying groceries, tracking expired food, completing house projects, cutting the grass, etc.

Whatever arrangement you have will need modified when the baby arrives. As you have discovered, or soon will, babies are all-consuming. Not only does someone need to be on top of direct care and supervision, but also the number of tasks needing to be done increases exponentially.

You and your husband each have a set of preconceived notions about how your growing family will operate. Chances are, you aren't on the same page. The single greatest source of disappointment and frustration in any context hails from expectations failing to be met. It's the reason I wrote this book. Realistic expectations set the stage for joy and contentment. Unrealistic or uncommunicated expectations will detract from this awesome stage of life.

There is no greater need for expectations to be clearly communicated than in the vision for the family unit. This vision can only become reality by aligning with your partner on a very detailed division of labor (DOL). To successfully accomplish this, both you and your husband need to start with a solid understanding of how your child will alter the demands on your time and energy.

All-Consuming

It is hard to fully internalize how all-consuming a young child is. Someone must be on duty or on call Every. Single. Second. Of. Every. Single. Day. For years.

Someone has to be on call to fish the pacifier out from under the crib at three in the morning. Someone has to sooth the gassy tummy, change the blow out, wait for the rump to fully dry, and apply the diaper cream. Someone has to overcome baby's startle reflex when transferring her from arms to crib, and try (for the third time, at eleven o'clock at night) to get her back to sleep. Someone has to be in charge of rocking your child until your ultra-considerate neighbor concludes his midnight fireworks display throughout the month of July. Someone has to be in charge when your kiddo reduces his Saturday nap by an hour. Someone has to clean up the puke when your child catches a stomach bug. Someone has to be on point when he wakes up at five-thirty in the morning, when he is put to bed at night, and supervise every minute in between. Saturdays, Sundays, holidays. All the days.

I'm belaboring the point because it's really hard to grasp until you live it. The 24/7 supervision intensifies when baby becomes a toddler who can now move about the house, climb over the crib, scale the dresser, get on top of the TV stand, and empty every drawer within reach prior to hopping into the dryer—all while maintaining his oblivion to danger. Littles do not understand that glass things break, bookcases tip over, stoves are hot, gravity will play an unwelcome role in their staircase descent, or streets are for fast-moving cars operated by the most distracted drivers in history.

God designed marriage to be a team effort all the way around. There is no greater setting where it is critical for all players to bring their A game and come having solidly studied the playbook. I hope this chapter will give you a strong start at creating or updating that playbook for your unique family. A clear plan (which should be fluid) is key to satisfaction and harmony as you and your husband adjust to the new life stage you have just entered.

Unspoken Expectations Don't Work

According to Pew Research, only thirty-eight percent of women say they are very satisfied with the way household chores are divided up. The study also noted that when it comes to child-rearing, women see themselves carrying a much heavier burden than their spouses. As previously noted, there is a massive spectrum upon which men fall in their openness to take on work that our mothers and grandmothers handled. Many of his expectations will be influenced by the examples he had while growing up. Consider this as you work with your husband on the best plan for your family. You need to understand what he believes your respective roles in the family will be. Expectations are everything. Understand his and be overt about yours.

You may have gathered by now that there is a lot I goofed up on in my transition to motherhood. I didn't realize it at the time, but looking back I can see I had a ton of expectations of my husband (and he of me) that neither of us shared with the other.

What I Imagined

He would get home from work by six in the evening, at which time I would transition from daytime caregiver to co-parent. He would have dinner with us and share in cleaning up dinner, giving baby a bath, putting away toys, brushing teeth, reading a story, comforting the baby if she was upset, and any needed household tasks. We would take turns a day or two each week enjoying a break while the other covered the evening responsibilities. We would equally co-parent on weekends and holidays.

What He Imagined

My husband had expectations that our home would run along more traditional lines: He would bring home the bacon; I would do everything else. In his mind, my part-time employment was optional.

I was especially perplexed at his expectation that I would handle things like RSVPing to his friend's wedding, or planning, purchasing, and wrapping Christmas presents for his entire family. As noted, he fell on the laggard end of the aforementioned adjustment scale. My husband is loving and very dedicated, but this did not prevent our opposite views from causing massive problems.

What Actually Occurred

My husband's job was never of the eight-to-five variety, and the birth of our daughter did not change that. I only added to his stress every time I complained about his minimal presence for evening duties. My part-time job provided me with a needed baby break; however, it was on me to manage it along with full domestic responsibilities. The line between my daytime job as mom and us co-parenting in the evening was nonexistent. Additionally, I was educated and experienced, and had ambitions of continuing to grow in my career. If I had extra time, which I didn't in the early years, I wanted to spend it on a professional endeavor, not preparing nightly homecooked meals, ironing, performing home repairs, or other domestic chores that would make his life easier. He thought I would be happy taking care of our child and home, without the worry of an outside job. And, he thought that in relieving me from financial concern, he would be off the hook for all adult responsibilities outside of employment. He thought I should take care of everything from our daughter's care and developmental needs, to yardwork, to keeping the water softener filled with salt, to ensuring that our insurance was current—and everything in between. We were not aligned on our family vision.

Disappointment on both sides began oozing everywhere in our home. Some of his expectations offended me. Didn't he know what a hassle it is to load up the baby gear and carry a pile of his clothes along with a ten-pound infant seat, occupied by a twenty-pound baby, into a dry cleaner? He could pop in and out, blissfully solo, in three minutes. And on his end, my husband's frustration was evident when I asked him to rake the leaves or clean out the garage during his weekend "nothing box" time.

Resentment Creep

An unclear division of labor can add to the resentment risk noted in the previous chapter. One night, I called my husband at the office to check in. (OK, fine, I was calling to see if he was getting his rear end in the car anytime soon because I wanted him to give our kid a bath while I handled dinner.) He informed me he was out having a drink. I do not know how to convey in writing the long pause and extreme level of ticked-off that I was in that moment. It had not entered his consciousness that he had extended the toughest part of my day (evenings) and upped my working hours from twelve to fourteen (night-time wake-ups not included) without so much as a discussion. He never viewed himself as having any evening parenting responsibilities. And why would he? We never talked about it.

My bitterness only built as this dynamic played out further: I did not have the luxury of walking out the door to have a drink (or do anything else) at the end of my workday. If I wanted to go out, it was *work*. It was work to reach out to two or three babysitters (which I had already identified and vetted) and book one in advance. Spontaneity was a thing of the past. I then had to inform the babysitter of any meals that needed to be administered, cleanup and screen-time expectations, bedtime routines, and general household rules before departing. On top of all that, I was managing safety concerns, sibling arguments, and about a dozen "mom" requests while trying to fix my hair and remember how that YouTuber told me to achieve the smoky eye. Feeling that your husband doesn't "get it" and isn't carrying his share of the load will fire up the resentment coals if you don't get out in front of it.

Communicate Expectations

Your family's situation will be different, of course. But I guarantee that both of you have expectations. Leaving them unspoken will lead to conflict. So, figure them out! It's the first step.

What Do You Expect of Him?

What are your expectations of him as a dad? Do you think he should spend quality, electronic-free time with your child? How much and how often? Do you expect him to participate in evening supervision? Do you expect him to help with housework, cooking, changing diapers, ensuring your child has the correct-sized boots for winter, clipping nails, shopping for Christmas, scheduling or attending doctor's appointments, giving baths, or any of the other multitude of tasks I lay out in the division of labor (DOL) list noted at the end of the chapter?

What Does He Expect of You?

Talk with him about his expectations of you. Does he expect you to continue to contribute financially or does he want you to pull back on your career to take care of your child? Does he view childcare as an easy task that you will readily handle into the evening hours? Does he expect you to keep the bathrooms stocked with toilet paper? Does he want you to parse through the important versus junk mail your family receives each day? Does he expect you to be the primary host when his family visits? Does he assume you will handle creating family photo albums?

Hopefully you can begin to see why going through the very detailed division of labor document I provide will help your family run much smoother than if these considerations are not taken. This document is noted at the end of the chapter for reference; however, I highly recommend you download it from my website and work through it together with your husband. This also allows you to revisit your agreement and modify it to best fit your family needs as they evolve over time. The document can be found at lori-arnold.com/book.

Taking Expectations a Step Further

While it is the seemingly little tasks that become thorns for a new mom and dad, there are much bigger questions to consider as well:

- What kind of schooling do you and your husband wish to pursue for your child, whether homeschooling, public, or private?

- How do you expect discipline to be handled in your family?

- Who is going to be the family prayer leader?

- What kind of family traditions, whether big or small, do you want to establish?

- What do you want your family life to look like? (How does this align, or not, to your husbands' vision for the family?)

- What values do you wish to instill in your child?

As time goes on and your child grows, the needs of your family, both big and small, may very well change. Any number of dynamics can change even the best-laid plans. The key is to have a collective plan and adjust it together as often as needed.

Lead from the Neutral Zone

The second step after communicating expectations is to lead from the neutral zone. He is not wired with the interconnected foresight skills you have. Remember his individual boxes that don't touch? He will hopefully be a wonderful partner in this new parenting world. But you must be the director. In another episode of "it's just the way things are," we women must make these connections happen. He won't see what you see.

I didn't do this. I fought it. I told myself, *He's a grown adult. These are his kids too. I have enough on my plate without having to manage his domestic engagement.* Not only did my resistance get me nowhere, it made our family situation contentious and plain unfun.

As your invested, want-the-best-for-you, biggest cheerleading, fellow mom, I say: Ditch the desire for fairness and initiate the positive change. Unloading on your husband in a frustrated rampage will not result in the desired outcome. I speak from great experience.

Be a leader in establishing regular neutral-zone connections with your husband. A mom truly is the heartbeat of the family. Your mood, attitude, and demeanor have a major impact on your husband and children. Set yourself up for joy.

Connect During Regular Neutral-Zone Chats

We know and understand our own realities to perfection. We live them. We know how our energy levels are trending, how difficult our days have been, and where our pain points are. Not only can we communicate these to our husbands during neutral-zone chats, but scheduling regular check-ins will also give us the opportunity to better understand *his* realities.

This is a good time to pause and reflect on the wisdom of Emo Philips, who said, "Never judge someone until you've walked a mile in his shoes." Recognize that your husband does not have the ability to fully understand all the magic you perform and mayhem you endure as a mom. We must be humble enough to recognize the same.

I made the rookie mistake of thinking that my husband's life was basically unchanged by the birth of our daughter, while mine had been turned upside down. He continued to go to the same job and keep the same hours as he did before she arrived. Even his weekends didn't look terribly different. I failed to recognize that even though his job was unchanged, he had internalized a massive increase in his responsibility as a provider and protector. He took on extra stress and concern for taking absolute phenomenal care of our family.

Your husband will, too, even if you contribute wholly or partly to the family finances. Providing and protecting are in his DNA. Recognize this and appreciate it. Verbalizing your understanding of his concern for you and your child will make him the happiest husband imaginable. Because the family workload has increased so dramatically, it may feel like things are imbalanced, when in fact, both of you are taking on as much as you can handle.

Make sure to ask: How are things going for him? How are his energy levels? What is causing him stress? Often, when we gain a better understanding of his unseen load, it becomes easier to carry our own. Just like he won't see *all* that you handle on a daily basis, you won't see everything he is taking on.

Regular connection allows you to halt ruminating thoughts of perceived unfairness and operate under a plan rooted in reality that works for the family unit. It also helps to foster appreciation, which is one of the most uplifting gifts one partner can give another.

How to Share Work

Now that you are firmly grounded in understanding the importance of the division of labor, let's get into the details of how to partner with your husband now that your precious baby has been added to the mix. If you are already headed toward toddlerville, but have not had this detailed discussion with your hubby, do it! It is never too late! You have years of partner parenting ahead.

Make Agreements Tangible

I have created a detailed list of tasks that need to be divided up between you and your husband. This can be found at the end of this chapter and downloaded at: lori-arnold.com/book. Most people will skip over this. *Please* resist the temptation to skip this. I promise printing this document and using it to have a meaningful conversation with your husband will change your life for the better. The items listed are things that need handled outside of regular working hours (as defined by your family), whether on a payroll or at home with baby. Or, if one or both of you works from home, perhaps you agree to include some of these tasks within the realm of the day job. It's your call. Your family is unique and thus this list is not all-inclusive. Add what you need to. Change the categories. Make it work for you.

Working through these items in great detail will drive clarity and prevent a backend blowup when they present themselves as "to dos" without a clear owner. Your family DOL game plan should be put *on paper* and it should be crystal clear who is responsible for its completion. If that task is to be outsourced, make a note of the person in charge of overseeing its execution.

Recognize that tasks are different in time, effort, and tolerance. There is a lot to divide and conquer. Make an agreement. Putting it on paper will increase your family's harmony.

Focus on What's Important

Here's a strategy I love that may help as you divide up tasks: Match up tasks with things your husband cares about. For example, if it's important for him to be on time, put him in charge of getting the baby and the diaper bag ready for church and other family outings. If he is particular about the food available in the house, perhaps he's in charge of meal planning and grocery shopping. If he loves having friends over, he takes the lead on hosting tasks.

Speaking of visits, discuss the frequency and expectations around family visits and trips. Leaving the house for a weekend is now a much more complex endeavor, especially the departure and return. I unloaded on my husband more than a few times when he would hit the couch as soon as we returned home on Sunday afternoon. (He had missed his "nothing box" time and was now trying to get some in!) Meanwhile, I got to work unpacking, getting dinner together, starting the laundry, and playing catchup on meal prep and other tasks that needed to be done—all while supervising our young, danger-oblivious child and stewing in frustration. A proactive discussion would have been a far superior approach.

If you want to dive deeper into the topic of division of labor, I recommend *Fair Play* by Eve Rodsky. This book and accompanying card game is devoted to the universal, enduring issue of women becoming the "shefault" parent responsible for all aspects of a busy household. The notion that Mom should have no problem independently covering evening supervision, making and cleaning up dinner, tidying up toys, handling bathtime, brushing toddler teeth, saying prayers, reading stories, and anything else involved in the bedtime routine, night after night, is sheer nonsense. That nonsense turns to madness if you add a second child.

Regardless if you are an unpaid champion or paid MVP mom, parental responsibilities need to be clearly established so both parents know who is in charge of what, and when. This includes early mornings, evenings, weekends, sick days, snow days, holidays, and vacations. If you are transitioning to champion mom, be sure to discuss when your job of daytime caregiving ends and evening co-parenting begins.

Whenever possible, regular evening and weekend participation from *both* parents is better for everyone, especially your child. It allows for more laughs, more teaching instead of yelling, and more time to enjoy these irreplaceable moments when your child *wants* to sit on your lap and snuggle.

Remain Flexible

If you are transitioning back to your previous career, leverage the division of labor document to modify any previous arrangement. Moms tend to be the go-to for many household tasks during maternity leave. As your time at home shifts, so should your agreement with your husband.

If both parents are returning to outside employment, make a plan for how to choose a care provider and agree on who will own drop-off, pick-up, packing meals and supplies, cleaning bottles and lunchboxes at the end of the day, sick days, school closures, and management of all daycare communications.

Not to be overlooked, make a point in your DOL plan to carve out time for joy and personal fulfillment. Eve Rodsky calls this "unicorn space." Discuss what you each need for your own happiness. If one person recharges alone, alone time should be built into the schedule. Many unpaid champion moms are not fully satisfied focusing on caretaking and household management alone. Some want nothing more than to care for their family. Talk about what matters to you. Time with friends, the ability to sleep in, exercise, a side-hustle, or whatever joy-sparking activities look like to each of you, be sure to build those into the family plan. It can be all too easy to become absorbed in the unavoidable responsibilities of daily life. You and your husband should help each other create space for the things that bring you joy. On this note, recognize the difference between verbal support and tangible support.

Walk the Talk

My husband has always been unbelievably supportive—in words. Tangible actions, however, were not always present to back them up. He would regularly show excitement when I acquired a new personal training client, and he would happily offer a connection to someone who might be interested in my blog. But when it came time to fold laundry or watch the kids on a weekend so I could work on these personally fulfilling endeavors, there was resistance. Being verbally supportive is one thing; taking on *actual* work so you can devote time to your outside job or hobby is another matter. Of course, the same goes for your husband. He needs bucket-filling time as well. You are in a rock-solid place once you both have agreed on the division of labor.

A quick shout-out is warranted here: Single moms, you have my sincere and deepest admiration. You are so incredibly strong. But, please, ask for help whenever and wherever you can. What weekly assistance can you solidify? Could a parenting swap be arranged? Is there anyone at your church that might be willing to provide childcare for a few hours each week? Can you find a neighborhood "mothers' helper" willing to offer free help in exchange for experience? Parenting was never intended to be a one-person job.

I recognize that many families have a working situation that does not allow both parents to be home on evenings, weekends, or holidays. Make sure to discuss how to partner in the below workload given the unique employment situation of your family. A job requiring a lot of travel or commute time will have a different impact on the DOL than one largely worked from home. A dual-income family will divide things up differently than a single-income family. A job of nine-to-five variety is different than one requiring sixty or more hours per week. Just remember that caring for a baby or toddler is a non-stop job in and of itself. Make the arrangement that works best for your family. Set the foundation for love to be the driving force in all the changes and challenges your family faces as you add this most wonderful, yet time and energy-consuming responsibility (the baby!) to your lives.

Self-Care and Soul-Care

I want to close this chapter by encouraging you to always seek the forest, though you are surrounded by many trees. While the "to-dos" will always look you square in the eye, put the less demanding aspects of your day first wherever possible. Doing so makes everything else more manageable. Life makes it easy to shift our attention to what feels urgent while demoting things of greatest importance. Self-care and soul-care should be high on your daily list; they matter significantly. Time with God, even just thirty-second prayers for mercy and grace throughout the day, keeps us grounded amidst the chaos. Walks, uplifting music, a quick workout during nap time, time with friends (even if interrupting kids are in tow) should take precedent.

Ok, time to check out the Division of Labor checklist that follows. This is also available in a Word document for you to download and make your own at: lori-arnold.com/book.

Set up some time with your teammate, grab a glass or two of your favorite beverage, add some yummy snacks, and get to work! It will meaningfully improve your relationship, your early mothering experience, and your daily happiness.

Next, we'll move out of changes and challenges to self and marriage, and into a heads-up on what to expect as baby moves through the early ages and stages.

Time/ Energy Required	Responsibility	Owner (The person responsible for the task)	Notes
Moderate time & energy/Frequent	Regular prayer time with your child (Awesome if it can be both!)		
	Uninterrupted snuggle time (I recommend a "both" here.)		
	Give child a bath		
	Brush child's teeth (After they come in, of course)		
	Cut child's finger and toenails		
	Child development (Ex. reading books and any priorities or special needs)		
	Put child to bed (For some, this can be quite a process)		
	Manage the family mail		
	Take out the trash/ recycling		
	Manage all toiletries/ cleaning supplies • Keep track of what is running low • Purchase needed items • Fill soap dispensers, stock bathrooms with TP, etc.		
	Pet care • Regular feeding/grooming • Scoop poop or clean litter box, fish tank etc. • Annual vet visits + sick visits		
	Lawn care: Cut grass, pull weeds, trim bushes, etc.		
	Water the plants		

Time/ Energy Required	Responsibility	Owner (The person responsible for the task)	Notes
Moderate time & energy/Infrequent	Child haircuts		
	Manage child(ren) well-check, dentist, and eye doctor appointments		
	Maintain correct size-to-season clothing, coats, gloves, hats, and shoes for child (Donate, sell, or store outgrown items)		
	Change lightbulbs, remote control batteries, etc.		
	Change smoke detector batteries (Even if they are going off at 2am)		
	Purchase salt and fill water softener		
	Change HVAC filter		
	Manage semi-annual heating, cooling, and plumbing maintenance		
	Car maintenance or repair (Cleaning, oil changes, etc.)		
	Appliance maintenance (descale coffee maker, clean out washer hoses and dryer vents, change filter on vacuum, etc.)		
	Manage unexpected home repairs		

Time/ Energy Required	Responsibility	Owner (The person responsible for the task)	Notes
Significant time & energy/Frequent	Device-free child-choice time (Ideally this is both parents)		
	Joy-sparking activities for Mom and Dad		
	Child supervision (All hours of the day must be accounted for. You will benefit from a loose plan for the specific hours Mom or Dad is on point, along with family time.)		
	Daycare management, if applicable • Packing food and supplies • Drop-off and pick-up • Cleaning out bottles/ lunchbox items • Manage communication and special events		
	Meal plan/grocery shop (Includes keeping track of pantry & condiment inventory and knowing what needs to be purchased.)		
	Prepare, serve, and clean up all meals and snacks (Includes bottles and pumping supplies. May want to split up responsibility for cooking and clean-up.)		
	Laundry (Includes towels, sheets, living room blankets, etc.)		
	House cleaning (May want to divide specific tasks or make note of who is in charge of managing an outsourced provider.) • Vacuum • Dust • Sweep and mop floors • Clean bathrooms • Clean kitchen countertops, appliances & wipe down cabinets		
	End of day toy pick-up		

Time/ Energy Required	Responsibility	Owner (The person responsible for the task)	Notes
Significant time & energy/Infrequent	**Sharpen parental skills** (Research relevant topics based on your child's needs. How to address a specific emotional or behavior issue, track down answers to a development question, learn about potty-training techniques, etc.)		
	Address night-time wake-ups, potty or throw-up accidents, soothing needs		
	Plan and execute child's birthday party (Purchase and wrap gifts, invitations, decorations, house cleaning, plan, purchase and prep food, etc.)		
	Play St. Nicholas (Gift purchasing and wrapping is significant. Discuss how this will be handled for immediate and distant family.)		
	Celebrate other holidays (Purchase Halloween costumes and candy, buy Easter basket items, fill Easter eggs, etc.)		
	Manage family finances (Includes college savings, retirement, health, life, and car insurance, managing HSA or flex spending accounts, and filing taxes.)		
	Manage unexpected or incorrect bills, insurance issues, etc.		
	Manage household renovations or maintenance (Ex. painting, appliance repair, home improvement etc.)		
	Clean out the garage		

"Significant time & energy/ Infrequent" tasks chart continued on next page

Time/ Energy Required	Responsibility	Owner (The person responsible for the task)	Notes
Significant time & energy/ Infrequent	"Spring cleaning" outdoor and indoor (Define this for your family.)		
	Rake leaves		
	Plan the family vacation		
	Host family and friends (Wash sheets and towels, clean house if desired, plan, prep, and clean up meals.)		
	Manage the family memories/photo albums		
	Travel prep: Plan, pack, and unpack needed child items for trips		

Time/ Energy Required	Responsibility	Owner (The person responsible for the task)	Notes
Other			

CHAPTER 5

Daily Life in the First Three Years

As a young professional, I worked at a company where the employees rotated assignments every few years. The old joke rang true: "As soon as you feel like you know what you're doing, you change roles." Being a mom is just like this. As soon as the nap schedule falls into place, our child drops a nap and the schedule shifts. As soon as you feel your child is understanding a family rule, it seemingly drops out of her brain.

I might have made different choices (or relaxed a bit more) if I had known what changes were around the corner. This chapter is not about typical developmental milestones. Rather, it is a big-picture glimpse into how your daily life will shift as your child grows through the first three years. Of course, all children reach different stages at different times, so please know that these ages are estimates.

I include this chapter to give you a heads-up into early ages and stages, along with tips I garnered, to help you prepare for what lies ahead.

Newborn Baby: 0–6 months

- **Interaction.** Baby won't interact much with you in the
  beginning. Some refer to baby's first couple months of
  life as the fourth trimester. She should still be developing
  in the womb, but the accommodations had maxed out
  capacity. In these early months, you are feeding, bathing,
  soothing, laundering, diaper changing, and tracking sleep
  and feeding patterns. Baby cannot issue your paycheck by
  way of a precious smile just yet. I found that cuddles were
  enough pay-off for me during this time.

- **Nursing challenges.** Perhaps the number-one thing new
  moms are surprised by is the challenge of breastfeeding.
  First, whether to breastfeed is a judgment-riddled topic.
  If you choose to nurse, please know that it often does not
  go smoothly in the beginning. It's painful when your milk
  comes in, nipples can become cracked, the baby doesn't
  always know how to latch, and concerns about supply can
  loom. I encourage you to persist through the early weeks
  of these challenges if nursing is a priority for you. As my
  dad often jokes: "It'll feel better when it stops hurting." In
  all seriousness though, these challenges often resolve after
  a few weeks. Seek a lactation consultant if needed. If you
  choose to or must bottle-feed, know that the time spent
  washing all those bottle parts may feel unending.

- **Time spent feeding.** Expect feeding sessions to take quite
  a bit of time. For nursing moms, a single feeding session
  can easily take thirty or more minutes and newborns
  often nurse four to six times a day. Cluster feeding, when
  baby might feed every hour, is also common as baby goes
  through various growth spurts in the early months. At
  times, feedings may feel like another to-do; however this
  quiet bonding time is usually pretty precious.

- **Safety!** Safety is paramount with a newborn (and toddler). Be sure to talk with your pediatrician (not the internet) about topics like co-sleeping and where/how the baby should sleep. Many moms find themselves exploring any and all ways to get baby (and themselves) some sleep. Social norms are shifting. While turning a blind eye to doctors' recommendations in the name of sleep has turned out OK for some, it has been tragic for others.

- **Lack of schedule.** Irregular nap times dominate. Baby might nap for twenty minutes or three hours. Sleep is tough for everyone in the beginning. It takes time to get into a rhythm of sleeping and awake times because many babies have their days and nights flipped. (Your movements and noises provided a wonderful rest environment in utero. Comparatively, a bassinet is far too still!)

  After a few months, more regular morning and afternoon naps take shape. This can be very helpful in establishing a routine for the many tasks we moms must complete that don't involve direct caretaking.

- **Exhaustion.** You are still recovering and adjusting to a level of exhaustion you likely have never experienced. These early months are a precious time to hold your sleeping baby after a feeding. Pray for her. Admire her preciousness, his tiny hands, her innocence, his long eyelashes. Give yourself total permission to do nothing while your body heals and adjusts to far less rest than it is accustomed to.

- **Outings.** Because baby sleeps so much and so easily (like straight through a running vacuum), getting out and about isn't terribly challenging. They often sleep through much of the bustle and usually get back to sleep easily after being transitioned in and out of the car seat. This will change.

- **Appointments.** Pediatrician appointments are frequent and necessary to check baby's growth and get in those early vaccinations.

- **Reset expectations.** If you thrive on productivity, it's time to reset your expectations on what you can feasibly check off the to-do list on any given day. You are now taking care of a person who is helpless. You won't be able to knock things out like you did before.

- **Ask for help.** This is a great time to practice asking for help and interview a few babysitters to add to your bench.

- **Use the straps.** *Always* strap them in! My daughter showed no signs of having any significant amount of strength. The swing we had was very deep and I thought it impossible for her to have the head and tummy muscles needed to sit up and roll out. I was wrong. Praise the Lord, I truly believe her guardian angel caught her. Under the swing were hard tiles surrounding our fireplace. I can only point to a supernatural assist to explain how her head did not hit that hard surface at full force. Changing tables are especially hazardous if we turn away from an unstrapped baby for even a second. *Always* strap them in to every device that has straps, no matter how incapable they might seem.

As babies move through these first few months, it's awesome to witness their growth in working to roll, sit up, grab at things, and take in all that surrounds them. Notwithstanding the sleep or any colic-type issues, this phase is usually ultra sweet.

That being said, this might be the best, or worst, time of your early motherhood years; it entirely depends on your lottery draw. I remember a dear friend saying: "I hate the baby phase." Her first child was hard. There was lots and lots of crying and general fussiness for days, weeks, and months on end. When I had my first baby, I thought, *What was she talking about? This is nice.* But my baby was pretty relaxed. We happily cuddled after nursing. She took a pacifier and a bottle, and enjoyed her swing. Then I had my second—and then I understood. She never took a single bottle. She did not take a pacifier. She did not like her swing. She cried any time she was not in my arms. And, in the first few months, she cried if we weren't moving around, so I couldn't even enjoy holding her while relaxing in a comfy chair. People talk about "good" babies. This is what they mean. Some are happy and content. Others are not.

Growing Baby: 6–12 months

- **Interaction increases.** This can be a fun time with more smiles and laughs, reaching more developmental milestones (they're getting close to walking!), and more ability to interact. It's still impossible to keep your lips off of them.

- **Two naps.** They are typically still taking two naps a day, allowing you some time to turn off mom-mode for a short time and get some work done since your hands are free.

- **Illness is normal.** If they are in daycare, or you regularly attend baby-filled outside activities, the colds and various viruses will begin to infiltrate your house.

- **Feedings change.** You are in the throes of introducing solid foods. It's really messy and nerve-racking as your kid has mini-choking episodes as he learns the whole chewing, breathing, swallowing thing. Talk to your pediatrician about baby-led weaning. It was awesome with one of my kids, but not the other. It's fun to witness the expression on their faces when they taste something new and tease out their likes and dislikes. I found it helpful to put towels on the floor and use bibs my child could not easily rip off.

- **Grow your community.** For those transitioning to unpaid champion mom, you may find that you are experiencing cabin fever, feelings of isolation, and boredom. To combat this, explore playgroups or library storytimes. You can only read books, play patty-cake, build with blocks, and ask children what sound a cow makes for so long.

- **Defend nap time.** Naps are an absolute asset to maintain. Of course, they help your child get much needed rest. But, perhaps just as importantly, nap time is the only time of day you can switch brain modes and relax, or get other adulting done without simultaneous supervision. Baby becomes more easily awakened and may have a harder time napping while out and about. I recommend putting a "do not ring" sign over the doorbell. You may benefit from a more structured approach to running errands if you schedule them around nap times.

- **Prioritize your own rest.** It was about this time when my husband and I shifted away from our prebaby ways of eating out, going out, or staying up a bit too late on a Friday night. We kept to our prebaby life for a short time, but the compounding workload and exhaustion eventually moved us into official parent versus young-professional territory.

Young Toddler: 12–18 months

- **Tender moments.** Kisses still abound at every wake-up, after every diaper change, when the nightlight gets turned on, and countless moments in between.

- **Dropping a nap.** Kids often transition from two naps to one at this age, which shifts the daily schedule. While you don't have as much "free" time to handle household management, this provides more opportunities to get out and about without the risk of blowing a nap and having to endure a resulting toddler exhaustion meltdown.

- **Accept long days.** There is a reason "the days are long but the years are short" was coined and endures. Do not worry about feeling bored when supervising and playing with your child for a full day. This can especially be felt by champion moms spending all days of the week and weekends with your child. The feeling is normal and does not mean you aren't a stellar mom. Champion and MVP moms alike feel like they must finish a marathon of sorts before they can close out each day. When toddler grows into a young child, the years do in fact, get much shorter.

- **Reduce pressure on yourself.** MVP moms should take care to avoid another kind of guilt. You might miss some milestones as you are away from your child for much of the day. You also might feel a need to make evening and weekend time extra great. Know this simply will not happen on some days or even weeks, especially as your child moves toward age two. If you are making kid-choice time happen (discussed in detail in Chapter 7), you are doing great.

- **Weaning and hormonal changes.** For those moms who have nursed up to this point, it will probably wind down during this period as your child may bite or not sit still long enough for solid nursing sessions, which can impact supply. The end of nursing can bring with it feelings of sadness at the soul's recognition that your baby is no longer. However, it can also bring freedom.

  Know that some moms experience significant hormonal fluctuations when they wean. It can be an unexpected roller coaster. If you experience this, give yourself a lot of grace and communicate with your husband so he can be supportive. Also, seek help from your doctor if needed.

- **Embrace the simple moments.** The preciousness of your kiddo remains front and center. They continue to learn and explore every day. Watching them get excited over the bunny they spotted on a walk or learn they can pop a bubble renewed my motherly spirit. You continue to be the center of their universe.

- **Walking.** Children at this age are usually walking, which opens a whole new set of doors—literally.

Growing Toddler: 18–24 months

- **Curiosity abounds.** Kiddos at this age take on the job of explorer, and they take it seriously. A new, three-dimensional world is opening up for them and they must find out what lies behind every door, drawer, and cabinet within reach. If you ever can't find your child for a second, check in the cabinets!

- **Get ready to chase.** As growing toddlers become proficient on two feet, mom-mode leaps to the next level. Little ones just love running, especially when they are near a street, in a parking lot, or out of your reach.

- **Practice pivoting.** This phase tends to bring with it a need for agility and surrender. You may be out for a walk and get caught in the rain. One of dozens of viruses may hit your house, prompting a movie weekend. You may need to make an unplanned trip to the ER. A late-afternoon car-nap may result in your child joining you and your husband's preplanned movie night. An unexpected mud pile your child gleefully discovers may prompt an unplanned bath. Though hard in the moment, know that some of the best memories are made when the base plan gets tossed.

- **A new kind of tired.** The type of exhaustion you experience shifts. Hopefully, you are now getting some solid sleep, which is necessary because you need a ton of energy to keep an eye and ear on your little explorer at all times. Many moms find this stage to be pretty darn difficult. Your child has the physical ability to get into most things without the accompanying mental development to understand that Christmas trees can fall over or TV screens aren't for throwing balls against. This stage breeds the mom-realities of checking email and making calls only when your child is strapped into a high chair or car seat. High-chair time was my most productive minutes of the day. I am not kidding when I say that the first time I sat down on most days was around seven o'clock at night for storytime. I was on my feet the entire day. Here are two words of solid advice for this stage: Baby proofing. The more you put into this, the easier your life will be.

- **Your little shadow.** They follow you *everywhere*. This is why a *New York Times*–bestselling book by a group of mom bloggers was titled *I Just Want to Pee Alone*. (For what it's worth, there is solid entertainment value in this book, but only after you have some hard-earned toddler-time under your belt.) I personally enjoyed some evening chocolate behind the refrigerator next to the trash can in my garage during this time. When in public, you can't leave your child outside a bathroom stall alone. This gets interesting when they ask what you are doing while attending to your monthly cycle. In my experience, the only time they didn't follow me was if I attempted to sit down on the couch for a few minutes.

- **Personal preference rules.** At some point, you will receive well-meaning advice to get babysitters and continue on with date nights and evening events. Doing so is entirely dependent on your personal preference. If Grandma isn't nearby, finding trusted babysitters to help during these early years can be tough. Your child is moving constantly with no ability to sense danger or follow instructions. Young babysitters don't know how to ignore a dinging phone. Your child also cannot tell you how things went at the end of the night. If you are like me and find it more stress than it's worth, do not feel guilty about being a homebody for this season of life. Many couples shift date nights to daytime coffee dates or cuddling on the couch after the baby is in bed. On the other hand, if time out renews you, make it happen!

- **Communication struggles.** Another challenge lies in communication. Your child probably cannot yet speak with any kind of clarity. The babbles are not quite decipherable, and it frustrates our children to no end. I found that learning a few easy signs (drink, diaper, food, all done etc.) was very helpful with my first daughter. It was an excellent mechanism for us to work through what she needed versus escalating tears.

- **Joy in simplicity.** Simple joys we have long forgotten become new again as we witness the pure joy of our child playing hide and seek, ring-around-the-rosy, and duck-duck-goose. The preciousness persists. We are still their favorite person in the world. And the clothes you can put them in at this age are *adorable.*

Little Kid: 2–3 years

- **Talking increases.** The communication lane has now opened. What lags is our children's recognition that, even though we can understand them, that does not mean they get a "yes" to their many requests. Actually, there are dueling "nos" happening now. They continuously tell us "no!" They don't want to leave the park, wear shoes, or use a fork. We have to say "no" so much, we wonder if we are killing their little spirit. "No, we aren't having ice cream for lunch, wearing pjs to Christmas church service, or ramming our trucks against the wall." And no (pun intended), we aren't killing their spirit. "No," *ad nauseam*, is normal at this stage.

- **From redirection to discipline.** You begin to shift your teaching efforts from redirection to discipline. It's a bumpy time because their little executive functioning software (and thus their ability to learn appropriate behavior) is slowly and inconsistently coming online. I cover this in detail in later chapters.

- **Constant needs.** You will hear "Mom" no fewer than sixty times an hour, excluding nap time. This is not an exaggeration. They are still exploring, and they want you to join in their every need, thought, and activity.

- **Follow their lead.** You might attempt some potty training now. Books abound on methods. My only advice here is to pay attention to your child. Our kids can be pretty good at giving us clues when they are ready for things like this. If you set the little potty out and they are interested, that's a good sign. However, giving your child some extra time if a battle seems to be inevitable is just fine. I had great luck with potty training during the summer. We played outside all day, always with a little potty nearby. Outside is where the accidents stayed.

If You're Welcoming Baby #2

- **Bring the baby book.** Pack your baby book in your hospital bag. You have lots of downtime in bed and the memory of your child's arrival is ultra fresh. Your children might want to know their birth stories when they are older. How long were you in labor? When did it start? Any unexpected events? Take advantage of your time by writing everything down during your hospital stay.

- **Sibling bonding.** I cannot describe the joy it brought me to watch my oldest immediately fall in love with her sister. I know it doesn't happen this way for everyone on the day baby comes home; however, many siblings have a very special love and bond with one another. Among the community of my daughter's rare genetic disorder, GLUT 1, it is often said: "If you don't know how to interact with or help a GLUT 1 child, watch their sibling." For some families, this bond does take longer to form and that's OK too.

- **Let them help.** Older siblings can relish the opportunity to be a "big kid" and a mother's helper with their new baby brother or sister. Take advantage of this and have them fetch a diaper, grab a spit cloth, or make a funny face to calm their sibling. This can help your bond with your older child remain strong and help them to feel special and included.

- **Special toys.** Some moms have a special toy bin they only bring out when it is time to feed the baby. This keeps those items more novel and could entertain big sister long enough to feed the baby. (Remember, if your oldest is a toddler or very young child, they are curious explorers without the ability to sense danger or be a good rule follower. Letting them roam the house while you are immobile isn't ideal. Of course, some moms become pros at feeding the baby while on the move. I wasn't one of them.)

- **Age differences.** The age difference between your kids can have a huge impact on your daily life. Have you ever wondered why some moms share the *ages* of their children when asked about the *number* of their children? "I have two under two." Or, "I have three under four." If you add baby into the fold and your oldest child is younger than two, you are doubling feedings and diaper changes, and you now must supervise a curious toddler while caring for a baby. Moms share their closely spaced kids' ages because they want you to know the extent of their superpowers.

- **Dealing with jealousy.** If your children are three or more years apart, your eldest is potty trained or soon could be, which reduces diaper duty. A three-year-old can fetch things like blankets and diapers, follow some general directions, and play independently to a degree. However, older kids may also become more aware that Mommy's attention is no longer fully theirs. Some moms have had a challenging time with baby jealousy and some behavior issues as a result. While not a foolproof solution, I found it helpful to give a gift to my oldest "from the baby" on the day we brought her sister home.

- **Exhaustion, again.** You'll work through the sleep deprivation phase once again. This lack of sleep causes the same challenges as it did the first time around. Unfortunately, since you now must simultaneously care for your eldest who may be napping less (or not at all), you won't get as much quiet nap time to recoup. After the first few months, baby will hopefully settle into a nap routine that allows you to (try to) align everyone's naps for one bout of quiet during the days you are fully with your child.

- **Ask for help.** My greatest regret was exercising minimal patience with my almost three-year-old when her sister arrived. I remember this so clearly. She wanted to help put diaper cream on her new sister. I was exhausted and wanted no part of the extra mess. She was being the precious, loving child God made her to be, and I was squashing it. If you find yourself more short-tempered than patient with your oldest, take it as a clue that you might need to ask for more help. This stage can offer lots of opportunities to apologize. It did for me.

As with all things, your personality, the temperament of your baby, and your family situation will make your routine look different from another mom. If you head back to an outside job, your weekday routine won't shift as much since another caregiver will be with your child while you are away. If you are transitioning to full-time caregiving as a champion mom, give yourself time and grace as you learn what works best for you. A good friend of mine made it a necessity to take her kids somewhere every day. One day, Costco. Then the grocery store. A playgroup. Storytime at the library. A park. She needed to get out.

I preferred to stay in. Poopy diapers are much easier to change at home. Pacifiers don't have to be sanitized when they fall on the ground *(ad nauseam)* at home. Screaming doesn't draw attention when home. Feeding was much easier from the comfort of my couch. I was also a fierce protector of nap times. An impromptu nap in the car (almost always inevitable if the trip is not purposefully timed) slashed precious "get things done" time. It also increased the odds of a fussy baby and frustrated mom come evening. Of course, cabin fever did hit and then I'd venture out. Personality types aside, all moms learn how to pivot the day's plans quickly in these early years.

Avoid Comparison

As the ages and stages take shape in your house, know that at some point comparison temptation will creep in. You will come across another family with a child close in age to yours. That child will say the ABCs, count to fifteen, spell his name, or showcase some other knowledge that will leave you wondering if your child is behind. Social media will showcase an eighteen-month-old who is fully potty trained, a two-year-old who has saved enough money to buy a special toy, and a three-year-old riding on two wheels. Our children have been blessed by Almighty God in their own unique way and will develop under the umbrella of our love according to His plan.

Some children are intellectually gifted and will pick up on numbers and letters sooner than others. Some are physically gifted and will perform gymnast-like stunts on the playground that would send your child to the hospital. Some are artistically gifted and will color an impressive picture while your child might still be in the scribble phase. At this young age, children should have the freedom to develop on their own timeline. Kids have fun learning the sounds that barnyard animals make. That's the key: *Fun*. Any academic learning you would like to do with your children should be completely play-based. If your kid loves to sing the ABCs, wonderful. If they resist, don't push them. And please, ignore the kid next door who has the song down pat. Always default to your pediatrician for developmental questions.

Parents today, more than ever, are pushing their kids to achieve, both academically and in sports. I was once chatting with a neighbor who also had a three-year-old daughter. She was talking about the various activities her daughter was in, including gymnastics. I remember becoming alarmed and immediately enrolling my daughter in a gymnastics class. I thought I was late to the athletic-development party. Not only was the class pricey, but she was not ready. Her ability to pay attention and follow her teachers' instructions made the classes pretty fruitless. As a soccer coach of four and five-year-old kids, I can tell you that even at this age, many children are not ready for organized sports. If it's helpful to have activities that provide structure to your week and your child enjoys it, great! But never feel in these early years that your child will fall behind if he is not in an organized sport or activity.

I have had the benefit of interacting with many experienced moms of older children as well as college professors. I hear it over and over: Older kids are burned out and incapable of bouncing back after disappointment. From an early age, they were pushed towards our worldly view of success. From the get-go, embrace an individualized, slow-but-steady path to learning, and you and your child will enjoy the fruits later on.

I think if I would have had a better understanding of what lay around the bend, I would have garnered more enjoyment in the present. I would have also handled the hard days much better. The normal challenges of adapting to the care of a youngster through various stages wouldn't have knocked me on my face so many times. I hope a little foresight will help you manage these stages better than I did.

CHAPTER 6

Moms Can Do Hard Things

A common joke across the Midwest says: "If you don't like the weather, stick around a few minutes. It will change." That's motherhood. There is sunshine, storms, light rain, unexpected winds, rainbows, the bluest of skies, and some tornados. Motherhood is like getting caught in the rain at dusk while a brilliant orange sun peeks through the clouds. It is stunningly beautiful—but you are still getting wet!

Moms everywhere, including myself and my wonderful mom, nickname our children "sunshine." The God-created spirit you see growing each day in your child is miraculous and heart-bursting. This spirit shares with you cuddles, kisses, laughs, and wonderful silliness. There is something truly magical about seeing your babe witness the beauty of the world. Each time they become intrigued by a beautiful butterfly or the shape of a cloud, we get to pause and remember God's amazing work, which we've long been accustomed to overlooking. It is also unbelievably satisfying to see your child hit a milestone or showcase the kindness you have been working so hard to instill. These precious moments are irreplaceable. Of course, you don't need a book to tell you this.

What you do need is a heads-up on how all this wonderfulness occurs far from isolation.

There is a reason that memes including "Like a mother" and "I'm pretty sure moms are some sort of scientific experiment to prove that sleep is not a crucial part of survival" are everywhere. Early motherhood is hard in a way I only heard about *after* I was chest-deep in struggle. That's why I'm giving you a heads-up on the hard. If you know it's part of the package, it won't knock your legs out from under you. Hear me when I say it: *Do not be discouraged.* You are entering fresh territory, which is always accompanied by a learning curve. Remember, this is all about expectations. The better your heads-up on what's coming, the better you can deal with it, and the more sweetness you will enjoy.

Far too many moms struggle as the glorious, new-baby bubble fades. I don't want that for you. Remember that perfection is fantasy. We all have yelled. We all have regrets in some form or another. This is a new job. It's just as tough as beginning any other new job. You need time to learn. Give yourself an immense amount of grace. You care. You care enough to be reading this book. Your child is extremely blessed to have you. You are the most important person in her world. Your husband is extremely blessed that you are the mother of his child.

As I introduce common challenges new moms face, take the advice that looks like help and leave the rest. Carve your own motherhood path. Learn and adjust as you go. Your baby will fill up your heart even through the rough patches. Motherhood is a wonderfully confusing, frustratingly majestic process by which God makes us better. When do we get better? When we are challenged.

Taking on Motherhood Challenges

As we dive into the realities that await us in this chapter, it's best to pause here and remember: Anything that comes easy is not fulfilling. There is pride in working hard. There is great reward in working hard. There is a great satisfaction in taking on things that are hard, giving it your best effort, and seeing the fruits of your dedication. Embracing hard things sparks growth. Taking on hard experiences garners fulfillment. Diving into hard moments develops grit. Doing hard things, especially when external praise is lacking, builds character. This is why women in nursing homes everywhere proclaim their greatest accomplishment is their children. The hard things pave the way for the greatest things.

Thankless, round-the-clock caregiving requires a strong sense of self, a big-picture mindset, and strength from Almighty God. You have them all. With this in mind, here is a sampling of early child-raising realities that will build more grit and character than you might care for.

The cleverness of phase-names like "terrible twos" and "threenager" can undermine the severity of momming through these phases. It is harder than most think. Just knowing that eases the adjustment.

Children are impulsive. They are irrational. The challenge that surpassed them all for me was the *whining*. Kids want what they want, they don't understand "no," they become overtired or overstimulated easily, and they only know how to do one thing when they are unhappy: Cry.

Have you ever thought about why they do this? Understanding more about this helped me tremendously. In the book *Smart but Scattered*, authors Peg Dawson and Richard Guare note that children's frontal lobes, the place where executive functioning occurs, is only potential when they are little. Young kids literally don't have the software needed to remember things, handle emotions, or follow directions.

So, what do we do? We lend them our frontal lobes. We plan, remind, orchestrate, protect, soothe, comfort, and try to maintain our peace while helping their frontal lobes develop. The lack of control may be unfamiliar territory for us. Studying for a final exam is hard. But you can find a quiet place, sit down uninterrupted, and study. Until now, you have handled hard situations involving adults with some form of filter for appropriate behavior. Now, you are dealing with a child that has her entire development runway in front of her.

As Steven Covey notes in his bestselling book *The 7 Habits of Highly Effective People,* we must remember our circle of influence. Frustration looms when we try to influence things that lie outside our circle. As a mom, our circle of influence over our child is quite large, but it is not infinite. We cannot make our children eat, sleep, use the potty before leaving the house, or stop crying. We cannot prevent our child from keeping us up until midnight or waking us up at four in the morning. She is in control of all of these. Our lack of control over these daily basics coupled with a child's illogical brain is why moms describe their work as "conductor of the hotmess express," "circus ringleader," and "chaos coordinator." Here me when I say it: mothering a young child is next-level *hard.*

A major goal I have with this book, in addition to arming you with encouragement and helpful tips, is to create solid ground upon which you can build your motherhood expectations. So, here's some grounding!

Hard Things When They Are 0–18 Months Old

- Motherhood jolts you instantly into a state of sleep deprivation. Everything is harder when you are teetering between states of slight to severe exhaustion. Every. Single. Thing. The hallucinatory state this leaves you in touches every part of your day.

- You will face unexpected issues that will be magnified by inexperience. Babies have issues from tongue-ties and ear infections to gassy tummies or an uncomfortable diaper. It is so hard (and worrisome) when you have an inconsolable baby and you don't know what's wrong. Once, a baby cried endlessly to the growing anguish of her mom. Turns out, she had a hair wrapped around her toe.

- You'll go on regular sock and pacifier hunts across the house and around the neighborhood as they toss their pacifier, socks, and all other reachable, removable objects on the ground repeatedly.

- You will perfect the new mom army crawl. When checking on your sleeping prince one last time before you go to bed, he will move. This will prompt you to immediately hit the floor and silently army crawl out, ensuring your child *does not see you* and proceed to be up for the next few hours.

- Cleaning makes its way to center stage. Diapers, spit-up, blow outs, and extra laundry become the norm.

- As mentioned previously, nursing and pumping are challenging for many new moms. It's not talked about enough. Feeding is also very time-consuming in the beginning. (Some babies can nurse for twenty minutes per side!)

- Going out is no longer an action, but an event. You'll plan around nap and feeding times, and pack up what feels like half of your possessions before leaving the house.

- Dropping your kid off in any childcare situation the first few times is rough. It's unbearable to walk away, leaving your child in an unfamiliar room with unfamiliar people while he is screaming to high heaven.

- Once they begin walking, you cannot take your eyes off them. While you hopefully will be sleeping through the night, the tiredness that accompanies constant (and I mean non-stop for every minute they are awake) supervision is palpable.

- Kids get very frustrated (and thus resort to fit-throwing) when they want to communicate something, but don't yet have the words.

- Social connection decreases. The added challenges and interruptions that accompany baby, coupled with a baseline level of tiredness, naturally results in fewer meetups and girlfriend phone conversations.

Sleepless baby nights are accompanied by babies sleeping in your arms during the day. Snuggling with your baby, kissing his cheeks endlessly, and watching her do new things with each passing week gets us through the hard in this phase. The smiles, the laughter, and the delight in each new discovery makes it all more than worth it. You love deeply and it will carry you through. You can do hard things. At some point, you will ask yourself, *Is it supposed to be this hard? What am I doing wrong?* Be assured: Yes, it is this hard. And no, you are not doing a single thing wrong. All this hard is compounded by our inexperience. Know that your intuition is sharper than you might realize.

Our Mom-Gut Gift

Mothers are blessed with a distinct intuition. I call it "mom-gut." Even the newest of moms can quickly recognize potential danger a foot away from the baby or anticipate what's about to happen when they see the wheels in their child's head turning. When insecurity creeps in, take a moment to listen to that still, small voice. I wish I had.

When I was pregnant with my first, I had been told that new moms freak out over every little thing. Remember the Luvs diapers commercial? "Live and learn, then get Luvs." Anyway, I foolishly went out of my way to avoid being one of those new moms. My baby had some signs that weren't typical for newborns. Of course, I wasn't sure what was normal, but some things did strike me as odd, including some irregular eye movements when she slept or her inability to sit up at seven months. After a longer-than-needed road of delays, which led to various therapies, we finally figured out my daughter had a rare genetic disorder. If you think something is off with your child, ask your doctor. If you feel like your concern has not been adequately addressed, keep asking. I didn't pay enough attention to my early intuition in an attempt to avoid being seen as a paranoid new mom. Be the paranoid new mom! There is no downside other than a reassuring false alarm. Mom-gut is always there for you—in numerous ways. If you feel like a particular group of moms doesn't share your values, find another group. If you feel your daycare provider isn't diligently caring for your child, start shopping. Your inner voice is a gift. Use it.

OK, on to building more grit...

Hard Things When They Are 18 Months – 3 Years Old

As you enter this new territory, here is a glimpse of the hard you may encounter:

- Reactions are not situationally dialed up or down; all land on the disaster side of the spectrum. Whether their arm is broken or they don't want to wear socks, the reaction is the same.

- They will not sit still for a nail trim, hair trim, or anything requiring stillness.

- They don't understand the importance of, and thus refuse to do critical things. Once, my two-year old spiked a fever well north of one-hundred degrees at two o'clock in the morning. She refused to take any medicine. I sat, nearly in tears, trying to explain to my sick, illogical toddler that if she wouldn't take Tylenol, we were going to have to go to the ER.

- They will get five splinters (aka slivers) in their foot over the course of three days. Yet, the level-ten flip-out during removal will not prompt shoe-wearing. They do not yet understand cause and effect.

- In public bathrooms, they will use twenty squirts from the automatic soap dispenser followed by claiming fifteen paper towels. They will try to sneak not using any soap at all when washing hands at home.

- They will use any possible thing as a step stool, including easily burstable cartons of chicken stock hidden away on the bottom of your pantry.

- Kids don't know what "powering through" or "pressing on" is. When their ice cream falls on the ground, they can't accept the disappointment and move on. You'll be expected to sit in, and work through, every emotion with your child—no matter how seemingly trivial. I call these moments a "toddler traffic jam." More on this later.

- Your iPad screen will consistently be covered in sneeze, your refrigerator in fingerprints, and the bathroom mirror with toothpaste splosh.

- They will insist they can put sunscreen on themselves and then scream bloody murder as you carefully bathe them while trying to avoid touching the resulting sunburn. (From this, I learned that I must still assert a high level of supervision, even as my child begins to assert some independence.)

- The nighttime routine will take anywhere from twenty-five to forty-five minutes as you handle one last onslaught of requests for stories, cuddles, water, and are begged to listen to "one more thing."

- Things will be lost *constantly*. You will say, on a loop, "We need to put things where they go so we'll have them when we need them." It's quite a pickle when the coat is lost on a fifteen-degree day. You will be forever searching for shoes, gloves, hats, and other necessities, often left at preschool.

- They will spill *a lot*. And you will spill as you navigate around papers, crayons, and playthings with one arm. I vividly recall a bottle of wine breaking atop my homemade cookbook and a bottle of olive oil greasing up my entire kitchen.

- Your floors will be sticky. See above.

- They will break the battery holder on the TV remote, put holes in the wall, and knock over any glass item within their reach. They will probably lose the TV remote entirely.

- They will find the long unneeded training potty in the basement and use it, but not tell you.

Great Mom Quotes: "My favorite thing about being a parent is being constantly told I'm wrong by someone who depends on me for food, clothing, and shelter."

—Danielle

Quick pause: There will also be smiles, cuddles, silliness, and so much love to go along with all the trying times. Toddler tantrums are accompanied by love, snuggles, and the sweetest, non-Webster approved phrases you've ever heard. Instead of overhearing my husband and I talking, my daughter would say, "I heard Dad and you overtalking." Their interpretation of various situations will provide regular comic relief. And their little outfits are beyond adorable. OK, continuing on.

- You will bruise your leg carrying your child and her bike around the entire block after she gets tired of pedaling.

- Your children will partner up to make their own frozen cuisine of blended water and Fruit Loops, which splash and freeze their way down every crevice of your freezer.

- They will put their plastic cupcakes in your oven without you knowing. New mom tip: Always check your oven before preheating.

- A lovely gift box you received filled with paper-thin confetti will become "hay" that your children joyfully spread across your carpet to jump in, potentially resulting in you needing to—thrice—disassemble and unclog the vacuum.

- They will write on the walls, cut their own hair, use lipstick as a crayon, and find the Gorilla Glue.

- They will empty out an entire container of shampoo in the bath.

- They will (always) follow you into the bathroom and ask what you're doing when tending to your monthly cycle.

- They will crawl around on public bathroom floors right after you've washed their hands.

- Somewhere around age two or three, you will hear "Mom" dozens of times within a matter of minutes. This continues, a bit more sporadically, through kindergarten. Just remember, you are their world right now.

- After storytime, they will dig their elbow straight into your groin as they push themselves off of your lap.

- They will open the kitchen drawer directly into your pubic bone.

- They want to do everything themselves: pour the milk, crack the egg, get the cup from the high shelf, use the stapler, light the candle, etc. With each request, you must decide if this is a learning opportunity you're game for or if the pending mess will be more than you can handle right now.

- There is hidden treasure behind each cabinet and drawer. All items must be explored—and left on the floor wherever the exploring ended. Just remember, it's developmentally wonderful for your child to be curious and explore, despite being immeasurably frustrating for you.

- They will need to poop two seconds before you need to walk out the door. (But, hey, it's better than two seconds after!)

- They will poop in the bathtub, leading you to perform a second full-body scrub down and clean the tub at the end of the night.

I share these examples, both specific and general, to arm you with tangible expectations. When the crazy comes to your house, find comfort in knowing that it is all normal. Your fellow moms everywhere are standing with you.

Your Positivity Counts

On those days where poop literally hits the fan, I want you to know with complete confidence that it is hard, you are capable, and it is very normal to feel overwhelmed, exhausted, and overstimulated. I will be forever grateful to my mom who peppered our home with inspirational quotes. One of my favs is about attitude by Charles R. Swindoll: "It is more important than appearance, giftedness, or skill. It will make or break a company . . . a church . . . a home. The remarkable thing is we have a choice every day regarding the attitude we will embrace for that day. We cannot change our past. We cannot change the inevitable. The only thing we can do is play on the one string we have, and that is our attitude. I am convinced that life is 10% what happens to me and 90% how I react to it. And so it is with you . . . we are in charge of our Attitudes."

A big part of my struggle with these early motherhood challenges came from my attitude. This, in part, was due to a complete lack of understanding of what early motherhood actually looked like. I was very unprepared for the many changes, and thus met them with rebellion rather than acceptance. This book is a product of my desire to eliminate this black ice for you.

Gratefulness is the gateway to an attitude which lifts us up again when we are down. When I was up nursing for the third time in the middle of the night, I was able to turn my view from frustration to beauty when I thought about my friends struggling with fertility who would give anything to be up all night with a baby.

More Considerable Challenges

Of course, sometimes, you will just need to vent about all this hard. That is OK too. With a positive attitude in mind, I want to give you a heads-up on a few more changes that are substantial enough to require a bit more detail.

Cooking for Kids

Motherhood shined a light on many blessings I didn't recognize or appreciate when I was younger. This includes how deep love can run, our family and friends' loyalty through rough patches, or how nice it was to simply sit down and have a plate of food placed in front of me day after day. It is now our turn to cast these blessings onto our children, knowing they are not yet capable of truly appreciating these gifts. Your relationship with your kitchen will blossom alongside your growing baby. Meal planning, grocery shopping, cooking, cleaning pots, storing leftovers and tossing them out at expiration, and pantry inventory management are a revolving door and a double-edged sword. Cooking is a major time suck, but is important enough to demand some of your irreplaceable time and energy. It is our job to establish healthy habits in our kids, which is becoming increasingly difficult. Sugar is everywhere. We are busy. Kids are notoriously picky. Growing babes and their hard-working mommas (you!) need strong nutrition, which is absent in the vast majority of convenient pantry pulls and drive-throughs.

The great news is, at this young age, our child's diet is in our total control. We decide what they eat and drink. Still, it's utterly draining to cook a healthy-ish meal only to have your child complain endlessly about it. Day. After day. After day. It's hard.

Regardless of what your nutrition goals are for your family, when you add one or more children to the mix, expect to spend an unreal amount of time in the kitchen. You or your bench will plan, prepare, and clean up breakfast, lunch, dinner, and snacks each and every day.

As with anything though, *it does get easier the more you do it.* It will take some time and experimentation, but you will find some go-tos that everyone can live with. The more foods you introduce your child to when they are young, the more expanded palate he will have for his future.

Perfection should not be a goal here. Be intentional about the general diet you'd like for your child, hit the drive-through when you need to, and just keep doing your best. An eighty/twenty approach is a good one when it comes to nutrition.

A final note on the often-thankless role of household chef: Jesus sees your quiet service. He calls us to serve. He gives us example after example of humble service, from washing the feet of his disciples to healing a leper with the command to tell no one. It's easy to overlook, but you are providing a beautiful service each and every time you silently cook for your family.

Cooking and Your Hubby

When it comes to food, it's worth considering not just the meals needed for your kids, but also the expectations of your husband. Re-enter the neutral-zone conversations.

I have noticed that food is quite important to most men. As with household chores in general, men's expectations regarding their wife's role in the kitchen vary wildly. If he went straight from his mom's kitchen to always ordering takeout, his expectations of you may not be fair or realistic. Small children make cooking a real challenge. You cannot simply stop supervising them when it's time to prep dinner.

If your husband wants a time or ingredient-intensive meal, he needs to get behind the cutting board or take care of your child. Once your child becomes interested in screens, you can decide if you want to use screen time to avoid simultaneously cooking and supervising. This is an important topic to work through as part of your Division of Labor discussions. If your husband looks to you to wear the chef's hat, help him understand the multilayered challenge of cooking, especially while supervising a fussy baby or curious toddler. If needed, ask for his help, whether for specific meals, weekend prepping, or taking on childcare at dinnertime.

Additionally, as baby begins to eat regular food, there is a whole other person with food preferences to consider. As you add more children, more preferences emerge. I like Mediterranean flavors, my husband loves Mexican food, my youngest is still in the pasta (with the obligatory vegetable) phase, and my oldest must eat a highly specialized, medical diet. Cooking a meal that everyone is happy with is not my current reality. It will be a process to adjust the cooking as your family grows.

Illness Hits Everyone Hard

According to WebMD, kiddos will get between eight and ten colds per year in their first few years—more if they are in daycare. This can be quite concerning with a newborn, especially when their nose is plugged and they cannot yet effectively breath through their mouth, which is a skill they usually don't acquire until they are around three or four months old.

In those early months and years of gaining your mom-footing, know that illness is common. When they are very little, heightened concern, nighttime nostril-sucking, and a few extra visits to the doctor are typical. If they are in daycare or preschool, you and your husband will endure the challenge of flexing the weekly schedule to accommodate keeping your child at home. Adjusting work schedules last-minute has the potential to add strain to your relationship if you haven't previously discussed how, in general, you will manage unexpected child illness or daycare closures as a parenting team.

These viruses often filter through the family over the course of several weeks. Just when I had finished nursing my child back to health, I would often start feeling terrible myself. Upon my recovery, my husband would take over the couch for the weekend. Of course, it will seem these bugs hit right before the family trip or the birthday party. My advice: Keep your kids out of all extracurricular activities a week ahead of a big vacation and buy trip insurance in those first few years. Expect various viruses to set up camp in your house for several weeks at a time in the first few years of motherhood. Plan accordingly so it doesn't completely take the wind out of your sails when it happens—again.

The Whining-to-Words Transition

Watching our children hit those first milestones is so exciting. The first time they smile at us, the first time they laugh out loud, the first time they roll over, crawl, cruise, and then take that first step are cherished moments. Verbal skills develop over time, just like physical growth. I was poorly prepared for this verbal development period, and thus it was the hardest for me to deal with. I call it the whining-to-words transition.

I had no idea how low my tolerance was for crying. Baby crying. Toddler crying. Little kid crying. All of it. Kiddos learn words one sound at a time. It can be extremely difficult for a child to deal with the frustration of not having anyone understand her. (Don't we all just want to be understood!?) It's actually amazing the things you will understand via hand gestures and various tones of groan. Moms are often the only ones who can decipher what their child wants in the early months of language development.

Still, two, three, and even four-year-olds revert back to all they have known since exiting the birth canal: Crying. We have to lovingly, and *ad nauseam*, teach them to "use their words!" We adults understand that not having enough milk in our cereal or not being able to go first when playing a board game is no cause for tears. Little ones do not understand this. In their world, little things are big things. Kids cry and whine a massive amount in the first few years as we teach them how to deal with frustration, disappointment, and tiredness. Of course, if your child learns that whining and crying equals compliance from you, it will never stop. This means that rather than giving in to *make it stop!*, you have to tell your child to "try again" by using their words.

The whining-to-words transition sucks the life right out of you some days. I never knew it was possible to love my kids with all my being and simultaneously want nothing to do with them. But it wasn't that I wanted nothing to do with them. I just needed freedom. I needed a break from the irrationality, the impulsivity, and the unpredictable. I hope you are beginning to see why self-care (and the help needed to make it happen) is critical.

The Kerplunk Effect

Have you ever played Kerplunk? It's a game where you thread plastic sticks through a cylinder and put marbles on top. Players take turns removing one stick at a time, trying to let the fewest number of marbles fall as possible. In the toddler-to-threenager stage, we moms get to play Kerplunk every day. Your patience is the marbles. The sticks are a whine, a spill, an ignored command, a broken object, a delay getting out the door—you get the idea. At the beginning of the day, a few sticks of whining and lost shoes are pulled, but no marbles fall. Pleading for snacks one hour after breakfast and the twenty-fifth mom-request of the hour removes a few more sticks. Perhaps a few marbles fall, but you remain in full control. Menu complaints at lunchtime, countertop-climbing, a refused nap, and getting poked straight in the eye leaves the entire game hanging by a single plastic stick. And then—that stick gets grazed.

The Kerplunk effect is the precise reason a staple motherhood term is "survival." It's the whining from the time their foot hits the floor because they don't want a "long day" at daycare *plus* they can't find their favorite shirt *plus* they spill the milk *plus* you realize you're down to the last roll of toilet paper. And sometimes the dog finds that mud spot in the yard and tracks it in just for fun. Moms near and far have all had a time (or several) where they broke.

I will never forget the time my spirit was sliced into pieces. It happened when my oldest came down with a stomach bug that lingered for seventeen days. That's right. Two weeks and three days. It started with the squirts that I had to clean up during the day. Then, she started hurling every night sometime between eleven-thirty and two o'clock. My subconscious would not let me sleep until after it occurred because I knew it was coming. She wasn't old enough to hit a bucket, so after she got sick, I started the cleanup, which included not only scrubbing bedspreads and carpets—and sometimes bathroom cabinets—but also included a bath in the middle of the night. The kids maintained their usual wake-up time of six in the morning and the TV was not yet a reliable babysitter. The compounding loss of sleep intensified my worry-filled days. A few days in, my youngest caught the bug as well. Mornings were filled with washing sheets and bedspreads and hanging them out to dry for the next nightly round.

As the days passed, my concern grew. Is she hydrated enough? Should I try to get her to eat? I made multiple trips to the store for Pedialyte. Halfway through her illness, I collected a diarrhea sample, loaded up the kids, and dropped it off at the doctor. The daily tasks of managing a household continued alongside nursing sick kids. The tiredness was growing hysterically with each sick-filled night. I believe it was on day twelve that I broke. After the tenth night of being up until puke-time (which that night was around one o'clock), cleaning it all up and getting back to bed, my youngest decided it would be a fine morning to get up at a quarter to five. I was in a state of utter defeat when awoken that morning by my twenty-six-month-old alarm clock, which was void of any semblance of a snooze button. I didn't sob. I squealed in a series of uncontrollable high-pitched intervals between shallow breaths. "Mommy is having a really hard time" was the only explanation I came up with for the kids who were wondering why their mom was losing it. I took a minute. I breathed. And I went downstairs and got breakfast started.

The seventeen-day stretch ended with me and my two kids in a small, windowless emergency room (where bloodwork was mishandled and repeated) with only a few granola bars in my backpack for our eight-hour adventure. During this time, my husband was right there with me (albeit with some breaks in order to keep his own dinner down). But, even with his help, the situation was within an inch of what I could handle. On some nights, we each simply cleaned the puke from one of the two kids, working out who would get the bathtub first.

This is the sacrifice of motherhood. I didn't want to clean up vomit. I didn't want to do extra laundry. I didn't want to collect a diarrhea sample and drive it to the doctor. I didn't want to make special trips to the store for Pedialyte. I didn't want to lose all that sleep. I didn't want to get out of bed that morning my toddler woke me up. I didn't want to spend an entire day in the ER. But I did, and you will too. We do it because we are strong, we handle what needs handled, and we love so very deeply.

I know another mom who broke after a series of days and nights with an extra fussy baby piled on top of standard toddler duties. She was giving one of her kids a bath while the other screamed her head off because she wasn't being held. Mom found herself repeating: "I can't do this. I can't do this. I can't do this." Thank God she had a wonderful neighbor who she was not too proud to call. The neighbor finished the bath and provided the calm and reassurance that was needed in that moment.

Know that we all reach a breaking point. These moments have nothing to do with your fitness as a mom, so never question that. You will get through these moments. You will see the light again. Never be too proud to ask for help when you need it.

Pulled in Opposing Directions

A final challenge I want to prepare you for is felt by moms everywhere. The requests of your child, your own genuine desire to spend quality time with them, and all the adulting that needs to get done will regularly pull you in different directions. There is *always* laundry to be folded, a dishwasher to be unloaded, mail to be opened, an incorrect insurance claim to resolve, a birthday card to send, a household essential to be fixed, an eye doctor appointment to make, a toileting situation to manage, carpet to be vacuumed, meals to be planned, groceries to be bought, food to be prepared, outgrown clothes to be sorted through, HVAC filters/light bulbs/smoke-detector batteries to be changed, a mess to be cleaned up, and on and on.

Even though I was mostly home with my girls when they were young, there were far too many days where I went to bed and realized I had not had a single moment of distraction-free, quality time with them the *entire* day. I hear lots of people talk about getting rid of mom guilt that often results from this conundrum. I think all our feelings, including guilt, are trying to tell us something.

If you are feeling pulled in too many directions for an extended period or if you are just not able to be the mom you want to be, step back. Take stock of how you are spending your time and brainstorm where you can adjust. It might just be a few extra busy weeks or it might be more. Perhaps a dedicated weekend activity solely focused on your kiddo is in order. Maybe you need a week of absolute minimal cooking. (I am amazed that my mom served cereal for dinner only once in my entire childhood.) At some point, you will feel you aren't spending enough time with your kid. That's normal. Make a change if change is needed.

Besides your level of help, your own personality and that of your child will factor into how easy or difficult a particular phase of child-rearing will be. I once had a mom next to me at the hair salon with her under-one-year-old sitting, not sleeping, *silently* on her lap the entire time. And the mom was getting highlights! That would have never been a possibility for me.

Strong-willed, defiant children are real. High-strung mommas are real. Children with special needs and attention challenges are real. Children who love to please are real, as are those who relish in leaping for joy across all boundaries. For all these reasons, and more importantly because God calls us to love thy neighbor, offer support over judgment for your fellow moms.

We don't know what other moms have been dealing with. We don't know what kind of defiant phase her kid might be in, what financial stress her family might be under, or what illness she has been battling. We don't know if it takes her three times as long to prepare every meal due to her child's special needs or how difficult it is to teach proper behavior to her attention-challenged child. *Always choose love*, because this mom-thing is hard. You will come across older moms who remember what's it like and offer support. And you will cross paths with those who won't hesitate to flash you the stink eye the second your child acts up at the grocery store. Offer the love. Reserve judgment for our Heavenly Father.

This Too Shall Pass

I want to pause and thank you for sticking with me. I think perhaps I was so unprepared for early motherhood because no one wanted to share the not-so-glamourous realities of life with littles. It is my truest hope that sharing this information will empower you to take on the crazy, and know that you are not doing a single thing wrong when it hits. Not a single thing.

If you're like me, you prefer to pedal your bike uphill first, then enjoy the downhill ride. During the can't-sit-down, tough, emotional-management days, know that the next phase is typically awesome. Your daily work through these difficult days will show up in a glorious way. Your child will regulate emotions much better and use the bathroom solo, yet has not been touched with any need to impress others, stress over academic performance, or had his spirit dampened by our broken world. The enhanced independence coupled with a continued unrelenting love of Mom is the best.

I suppose this is my way of saying "this too shall pass." Of course, when you're in the middle of the mayhem, this well-intended advice doesn't help. Despite this, try to picture dropping your eighteen-year-old child off at college. This sometimes helped me during those extra trying times. The fruits of our labor have a very long lead time. You must have an inner-knowing. Keep the faith.

Just like we believe in an Almighty God we cannot see, we must also know with certainty that every groundhog-like day and every challenging phase is bringing about the ultimate goal of developing your child into the adult that God created him to be, to fulfill the purpose only he can fulfill.

I want to close this chapter by encouraging you with the very same advice our Lord encouraged His people with throughout history: "Be strong and of good courage." This phrase is repeated time and again throughout the Bible. I want you, irreplaceable mom, to be strong and of good courage. Your own strength will surprise you.

CHAPTER 7

The Real Work of Motherhood

When someone has just accomplished something spectacular, they are often asked, "Who is the person you most admire?" The answer so many give without hesitation is "my mom."

"Strength and dignity are her clothing, and she laughs at the time to come. She opens her mouth with wisdom, and the teaching of kindness is on her tongue. She looks well to the ways of her household and does not eat the bread of idleness."

—Proverbs 31: 25-28

As we get older, we develop a deeper appreciation for just how much our mothers loved us, sacrificed for us, encouraged us, and gave us her everything. A mother's love is irreplaceable. You are irreplaceable. Grown children do not put their mom on a well-earned pedestal because she changed their diapers, washed their clothes, or cooked their meals. They deem her a superhero because of the example she set, the values she instilled, and the light inside them she nurtured through thick and thin. Therefore, we must never allow the necessity of daily caregiving, or all the hard we talked about in the previous chapter, cause us to lose sight of our most critical role: Teacher.

Our work as the primary educator in our children's lives spans from physical and psychological development to spiritual, emotional, social, and intellectual growth. We help them learn to walk, hold a spoon, use stairs, and catch a ball. We help them understand they are feeling frustrated or angry and how to cope with these feelings. We remedy toddler troubles, and model sharing and thinking about others. We teach them letter sounds, numbers, and vocabulary. We help them learn that bees sting, stoves are hot, and mirrors break. We teach them about Jesus and how to pray the Lord's Prayer. We insist that they be confident in who God created them to be, to love themselves, to embrace hard work, and to persist in working through problems.

In my home, when my kids were very little, my uptight personality and thirty years of only worrying about myself made it very difficult for me to take advantage of teaching moments. My patience always seemed to run thin, yet I had the burning desire shared by moms everywhere: To give my kids the best upbringing possible. More than anything else, I have come to recognize that parenting is a long game. A very long game.

One of the many amazing things about kids is how they learn and grow so fast. After only a few weeks, they are smiling, laughing, and grabbing. This quickly gives way to rolling, crawling, cruising, and interacting with you in the most heartwarming ways. They say kids are sponges. They really are. This includes our overt interactions with them, as well as the example we set as we go about our daily business. I began saying the Lord's Prayer with my daughter each night when she was about one year old. I didn't know if she was getting anything from it. One evening, a few months down the road, and after being seemingly oblivious to this nightly routine, she said every word with me! We then learned several more prayers. Before they can even talk, you will find them copying you. What you say and do from the earliest days makes such an impact.

With youngsters, repetition is the name of the learning game. Kids start out knowing nothing. Every situation and every nuance surrounding that situation is new to your child.

In my attempt to learn as much as I could in my new role as mom, I attended several parenting seminars. I distinctly remember one instructor pointing out time of day as a variable in the eyes of my child. For example, at breakfast, I told my daughter not to stand on the open dishwasher door. At lunch, she hopped back up. I told her again. After nap time, guess what happened? She hopped up again as I was loading more dishes. I was getting increasingly frustrated with each rule reminder. I now realize that she was trying to figure out if standing on it in the morning differs from the rules at noon or any other time. Now, multiply this idea by all the rules and all the nuanced scenarios in which you need those rules applied. Layer on the limited attention span of a child and you can see how frustration can quickly mount. I repeat: It's a long game!

As a mother, I adjusted to the need for repetition around tangible rules relatively easily; relative to teaching emotions, that is. Sustaining a teaching mindset when it came to emotions challenged me on a whole new level.

Teaching Emotions Is Tricky

It's second nature to pick up a book and read it to our child or ask him: "What sound does a cow make?" It's not as intuitive to put on our teacher hat when it comes to behavior. Just like kids need to learn colors and letter sounds, they have an even greater need in these early years to learn about emotions and proper behavior. The daily tasks a mom completes to keep the ship afloat can max out our capacity. Our baseline caregiving duties alongside teaching a curriculum which includes behavior and emotion regulation can leave our patience, understanding, and empathy for our child hanging on for dear life. To help shore this up, we first need to see our kids as real people with legitimate feelings they do not yet understand.

Even the smallest kids have feelings of sadness, happiness, frustration, pride, anger, anxiety, and everything in between. Although their instinct is to cry unless you agree to another occupant in your bed, they don't know that their feeling is called "sad" or that they are experiencing something called "anxious" about sleeping alone. We must teach our kids the names of their feelings, and of course, the proper way to deal with them. Frustration cannot look like hitting. Disappointment cannot look like meltdowns. During the learning phase, however, they do look like these undesirable behaviors. As we teach through these early years, often in a fogged-over state of daily child management, it's critical we recognize the learning curve our children face. Toddler traffic jams are the norm at this stage.

Just as we have no choice but to come to a full stop and inch our way through an unexpected traffic jam, we must also sit in, and inch through, typical toddler behaviors. It's extremely frustrating while we're in the thick of it, but we ultimately arrive, delayed but safe, at our destination. *Typical* toddler behavior is a key word. Many of these things can be truly maddening because we adults know they are no big deal. Going through a carwash is no cause for a freakout. Water running down your child's face at bathtime should not spark a fit. Thunder is no reason to be up for hours in the middle of the night. Kicking and screaming is not the way to leave a raging good time at the playground. Not-so-great behaviors are a normal part of a little human learning to be a bigger human. Toddler traffic jams pop up regularly. Take some deep breaths, try to see each situation through the eyes of your child, and do the best you can with whatever gas is left in your tank. The roadways will clear up as more time goes on. And remember, we all learn far more from our failures than our successes.

Moms Make Mistakes Too

A major new-mom blunder I perfected was yelling at my daughter after an innocent mistake. I recall a particular instance when she was playing with a ball. She kicked it and hit a friend in the face. "Look what you did!" I said, coming down pretty hard on her for not paying attention and hurting her friend. My reaction was driven by a combination of embarrassment, as I watched the other child's mom deal with her wailing kid, and my lack of patience after the accumulating challenges of the day.

My daughter was only two years old. She had zero intention of hitting her friend with the ball. She also didn't have the motor control or ability to anticipate the mishap. Rather than yelling, I should have taught her how to deal with her mistake. I should have helped her make sure her friend was OK and talked with her about how we can avoid this mistake in the future. I missed that teaching moment. I made her feel awful for a totally innocent mistake.

One day, God decided to bless me with some perspective when another adult absolutely laid into me for an unintended oversight on my part. She rolled her eyes at me and talked to me like I was a complete idiot. I realized how terrible it feels to have someone yell and talk down to me. It made me defensive. It made me furious. It made me lose respect for that person. Most of all, it taught me nothing. Our kids feel the same way when they are talked down to. If we are yelling, we are not teaching. Though never perfect, I now try to remind myself to give my daughter the grace to be human and make mistakes—the same grace we all need.

In addition to the yelling, I really struggled with tone. Exasperation frequently escaped my mouth. When I think of my young daughter being talked to like she is stupid, I cringe. I wouldn't tolerate anyone else talking to her like that. I won't tolerate it coming from myself either. A better approach is respectful or gentle parenting, also known to some as positive discipline.

Gentle or Respectful Parenting

Gentle or respectful parenting is all about recognizing and affirming our child's feelings, *no matter how trivial they seem.* These feelings are driving their (often unpleasant) behaviors. The goal is to understand the child's underlying physical or emotional needs, rather than dismissing these out of hand, and affirm them. Here are some examples:

- "I understand you don't want to wear your seat belt; however, it is important that we are safe."

- "I can see you are very upset. That toy does look fun, but we cannot buy everything we want."

- "You really didn't like that avocado. Even when we don't like something, we don't throw it on the floor."

This seems simple; however, it takes more effort and intention than you might think. Repeated infractions are a mainstay with young children. Dealing with the same situational meltdown or broken rule, again and again and again, can take our tolerance to zero. Unkind tones result. Yelling happens. Fail forward when it does.

Here again, God is guiding us toward growth. Being slow to anger (James 1:19) is a command I have not steadily followed. Being a mom gives us many opportunities to work toward this high calling. One thing I've gotten much better at when I feel my blood pressure rising is to overtly tell my kids, "I'm about to yell. I don't want to yell, but if that is the only way I can get you to listen to me, I'm going to yell." It's worked really well.

I remember receiving the advice to celebrate each meltdown my child had because each one was an opportunity to teach! I'm not sure about celebrating, but each misstep by your child is a chance to showcase big words, deep breaths, the feelings of others, safety know-how, and the like. We won't take advantage of them all, of course, but I have found this to be a helpful mindset.

I did struggle with the notion that affirming my child's every emotion would be counterproductive to giving her perspective. I want my kids to be grateful. I want them to understand a bigger picture beyond themselves. When my daughter threw a fit because her food was touching, I didn't want to affirm that. I wanted to teach her that healthy food is a true blessing. I've come to learn it can be both. Affirmation simply acknowledges our child's feelings. After all, feelings are feelings. Dismissing them does no good. I can simultaneously affirm by saying, "I understand you don't like your food touching" *and* provide perspective by offering: "Don't forgot there are many children who may not have any dinner tonight." Again, it's a long game.

Prevention Is the First Bad Behavior Barrier

Let's recap the initial aspects of our role as our child's number-one teacher: Lots of repetition, the need to guide our child through innocent mistakes and toddler traffic jams, and affirmation. But what about plain ole bad behavior? What is giving rise to it?

One challenge of momming is the fact that kids are so different. Yet, there are three universal needs all kids have: the need for power, attention, and sleep. When one of these is absent or lacking, negative behaviors surface. When kids are younger than two-ish, we are just redirecting all day long. As we enter the two-to-three age range, true toddler behavior patterns call for increased discipline and teaching. At this point there are two paths to consider: Prevention and consequences. This chapter will cover prevention, and the next chapter will go into consequences for undesired behaviors.

Before I get into how to prevent negative toddler behaviors, let me mention that most behavior issues with young children are tough, but totally normal. However, there are plenty of cases where professional help is advised. It can be difficult, especially as a new mom, to decipher challenging, yet normal, toddler behavior from behavior that would benefit from a child therapist. If your child is struggling with an issue for an extended period or if you don't know how much more you can take, there is absolutely no downside to seeing a professional. You will either get some much needed help, or they will assure you that all is well.

My wonderful MomCo (formerly MOPS: Mothers of Preschoolers) group shined a light on awesome child therapists and their creative approaches to dealing with bedtime troubles, managing anxieties, uncovering behavior-hijacking emotions, and helping kids through self-regulation challenges. If you've tried various approaches to a behavior problem and it's beginning to negatively impact your family on a regular basis, please reach out for help. As Peloton coach Jess Sims says: "No ego, amigo."

Give More Choices

The "power bucket" is all about kids feeling like they have some control over their little world. I don't particularly like other people telling me what to do. Our kids feel the same, yet we tell them what to do—and what not to do—all day long. Frustration and anger are often the result of our child's lack of power.

The biggest tip to avoid power-related outbursts lies in offering choices. Nonchoices disguised as choices work too. Examples abound, but here's a few that can be particularly helpful:

- "Do you want to go to bed now or in five minutes?"

- "Do you want broccoli or green beans for lunch?"

- "Do you want to pick up your blocks first, or your crayons?"

- "What book would you like Mommy to read tonight before bed?"

My personal go-to was a "by yourself or with Mommy's help" scenario. Here are two examples:

- "Do you want to get in the car seat by yourself or do you need Mommy to help you?"

- "Do you want to get in the bath by yourself or do you want Mommy to help you?"

Adult translation:

- "Do you need me to pick your tiny tushy up against your will and make you do the thing or will you cooperate?"

I must insert another all-kids-are-different caveat here. Parenting coach Meghan Leahy warns parents against choices. Some younger kiddos may become paralyzed by choices. They want to wear the red shirt and the blue shirt and maybe the yellow one too. If offering choices is not filling your child's power bucket, table this strategy until your child may be more developmentally ready.

Designate Them as Mom's Helper

Another tip on the power front is one that will pay off greatly in the future: Designate your child as an official family helper. Kids love being helpers and can do some chores at a younger age than you might think. You'll be empowering your kids to achieve the long game of independence and, over time, lighten your own load.

For example, kids will shove everything (including shirts, socks, spatulas, markers, etc.) into the toy bin unless they're taught to put things where they belong. An easy starting point as Mom's Helper is regular cleanup. If you happen to have the energy at the end of the day, you can use this as an opportunity to teach the value of doing things well, not just the bare minimum. Otherwise, an overstuffed toy bin is better than toy-covered floors.

Other things they could help with beginning around the age of two or three is feeding the dog or putting the silverware away. There are some great kid-sized brooms, mops, and even vacuums that can legit help with cleaning. Next up, attention.

Fill Their Attention Bucket

Kids need to know that they are important. They want to matter, just like all of us. Unfortunately, it takes decades for our kids to recognize the love we show them through the many ways in which we serve and care for them. They don't equate their clean laundry, full bellies, a joyous Christmas season, orchestration of their favorite activity (and on and on) with our love for them. Rather, we fill their attention bucket through our *undivided* attention.

When kids do not get enough of our attention, they begin to act up as a misguided tactic to get attention. If they are squeaky, they will get some grease. Even negative attention is attention.

Giving full attention can be a challenge. A MVP moms' outside employment is bookended by meals, laundry, baths, scheduling, and the like. Even on days I was not working my outside job, bedtime would come and I realized my child and I had not had any quality time. It was easy to allow a full day to pass having only tackled the transactional necessities of toddler care and household management. Adding to the more-to-do-than-time-to-do-it conundrum, our undivided attention becomes divided by our dinging phones, which are always within reach.

Another area where I got tripped up on the attention front was when I would take my kids to playgroups, the library, parks, etc. Upon returning home, I immediately got to work tackling the list of chores waiting. In my mind, I just spent a significant amount of time doing an activity *for them.* Mommy-and-me box checked, right? Wrong! The problem was, often, I wasn't actually giving them my undivided attention during this time. The library was fun, but we were engaged in the songs and stories from the leader more than each other. Parks were a great way to be outside and burn some energy, but if they were playing with other kids, or if I started talking to another adult or got on my phone while pushing them on the swing, I wasn't filling that attention bucket. The one and only way we can consistently meet our child's need for attention is through our *intention.* We must build time into the daily routine that is solely for our kids. It's even better if we make it "kid-choice" time. Here's how.

Kid-Choice Time

During this ten minutes, thirty minutes, or however many minutes you can manage, the tech is silenced and your child gets to choose (within appropriate boundaries) how she wants to spend Mommy-and-me time.

A caveat here: Do not allow "real quick" distractions. (I am the worst about this). Have you ever said, just when you've sat down with your child and started a puzzle together:

- "I'm just going to put the laundry in the dryer real quick."
- "I'm just going to put these dishes away real quick."
- "I'm just going to text this person back real quick."

As hard as it may be to do this, there are two major benefits to offering regular, kid-choice time. First and most obviously, they relish it. It will be their favorite time of day. As a result, many behavioral problems will be avoided because their attention bucket is full.

Second, it will allow you to tackle all your grown-up responsibilities without feeling guilty or pulled in various directions. The days when I fully engaged in an activity with my child left me with the guilt-free confidence to tell them "no" to the battery of requests they sent my way when I needed to get a meal together.

Outside of kid-choice time, I recognized I had a very bad habit of answering my kids while continuing a task and physically facing another direction. I now try to make a point of showing my kids they matter, and instill some patience in them by saying: "Wait just one minute please. I want to give you my full attention." This is one of my favorite phrases. I finish the dish I'm washing or get the last shirt in the dryer and then I make eye contact with them.

Prioritize Sleep

The final preventative measure to avoid negative behavior is prioritizing sleep. Our kids need a lot of it—eleven to fourteen hours. It will be blatantly obvious when this is lacking; instant meltdowns and an attitude of defiance are strong clues.

If you get home from outside employment and are having a hard time with your child, recognize that she may have had a restless day. If your child seems to be more combative than normal, think of sleep first. It's often the problem *and* the solution. Remember that we, as adults, are far more short-tempered when we are tired. Our kids are no different.

But what about if your child gets to the point of being so tired (and thus argumentative) that they refuse to lie down? It's a common problem and a common power struggle—and that makes it a double-whammy when it comes to dealing with our children!

"Never make eye contact with a child on the verge of falling asleep ... they will sense your excitement and abort mission."

—Mom meme, mummyhereandthere

Rather than engaging in a power struggle, get creative. Perhaps a choice can come into play. What five-minute activity does your child want to do before lying down? I often laid in bed with my kiddo when she refused to lie down by herself. With the noisemaker on, I would lie with her for five or ten minutes and then get up after she (nearly immediately) fell asleep. Of course, there were a few times I was not able to stay awake either; the laundry got folded another day.

If naps aren't happening, "quiet time" is a go-to strategy for nearly all moms I know. Try saying this, "You don't have to sleep, but we are going to have quiet time in our rooms."

The Value of Routines

Kids thrive with routines. It gives them a sense of security in knowing what to expect—and you already know that expectations are *everything*! It also helps ensure that things like sleep and attention are consistent. Snack times, mealtimes, nap times are all good candidates to schedule around the same time each day. Evenings are generally more difficult than daytime, and thus are a great time to have some predictable activities. What activity can your child expect while you are cooking dinner? (Hint: If under age two, this may be the time they spend in something that contains them, like a high chair, swing, Jumparoo, or baby-gated area). When is bathtime? What happens right before bed? For me, it was *Daniel Tiger*, a story, and prayers. It can be anything.

Prior to having kids, I was the queen of routine. After having kids, routines became harder for me. If my baby was on a string of restless nights, wake-up time varied. Some days, she would nap before the allotted time, or sleep half as long as normal. Illness always threw the system off. I encourage you to implement a solid, yet pliable routine knowing it will get shifted here and there.

I do have friends that were not able to make a consistent evening routine happen in their busy family, and that's OK too. It is just another tool to consider. The idea is to help your child know what to expect. This leads me to a related piece of advice I'd like to offer before we move on.

Just as I hope this book provides you with a heads-up, give your kids a heads-up on things they have not yet experienced. Kids can present challenging behaviors (e.g., crying, resistance) if they are taken by surprise, and in the early years *everything* is new. It is very helpful to tell your child, "This is an automatic toilet so it may flush before you're ready," or "The car ride will be longer than what we're used to," or "Here's how our car is going to get a bath" *before* your child encounters a new situation. It's especially helpful to give your kids a five or ten-minute warning before it's time to stop a fun activity. Some scenarios are going to be plain tough. Taking your child to get a shot is not going to be pleasant. You'll make the call based on the temperament of your child when a heads-up might be counterproductive. Even if you are a master at providing regular power, attention, adequate sleep, and preemptive information for your child, toddlers are toddlers. Bad behavior is part of the gig, and consequences are part of the learning journey.

*If you have already left an online review
for this book, thank you, thank you.
If not, doing so will make a big difference
in helping other moms find this resource.
Your support is deeply appreciated.*

CHAPTER 8

Teaching with Love and Firmness

Discipline is just another word for teaching. And teaching is the real work of motherhood. It's the main event in which you get to choose how the lead character (your child) will learn to slay the dragon (humans' natural temptation toward selfishness and mediocrity) by the end of the story (age eighteen). If your child is under age two, you can rest—from our tendency to worry if our child is going to be a good human, that is—in the soothing/redirection moment you are in. The territory of discipline is coming up.

Why devote time to talking about discipline when there are entire books dedicated to the topic? A few reasons: The singular goal I have with this book is to ease your transition in the early years of motherhood. The behaviors our children present as they (slowly) progress in their cognitive and emotional development can steal some of our joy in these early years. To meet this challenge, you need some tools in your back pocket. Also, I experienced some conflicting information as a new mom, and as a result, wavered in my own discipline journey. I want to help you avoid this. Some things transcend all when it comes to discipline, and I want to mention them up front.

Establish Your End-Game

When it came to becoming a mom, I had the most anxiety around discipline. As a result, I dug in. I attended multiple seminars, listened to podcasts, read books, and even took a course on the topic. The most impactful thing I took away, which I hadn't considered, was my end-game. I was challenged to overtly reflect on the type of child I wanted to raise and how my discipline strategy would enable that. Some questions I was encouraged to ask myself included the following:

- Did I want to raise little soldiers who obeyed every command, but did so out of fear?

- Or did I want to raise confident, resilient kids who know their voice matters?

- In choosing the latter, how would I instill this confidence while also ensuring they grow in humility, respect authority, and appreciate healthy boundaries?

My approach would need to look different from the "stop now!" discipline tactics I found myself leaning toward. A clear vision is your compass that will inform how you, with important consistency, will handle the many sticky situations kids put us in. It will direct you toward the bigger picture—to ultimately raise your child in a manner that enables them to be the man or women you hope they will be.

Calmness Reigns

As our child's life teacher, we must always try to remember that helping our children *learn* should be the foundation upon which we build our discipline strategy. In the spirit of teaching, know that there will be times when you have an able learner, and times when you will not.

The number-one thing I have kept with me from reading *The Whole Brain Child* by Daniel J. Siegel and Tina Payne Bryson is the idea of the upstairs brain and the downstairs brain. In short, our upstairs brain is a *higher* level of thinking. It is a place of calm. It is therefore a place where we can learn.

Our downstairs brain is a *lower* level of thinking. It is a place where we, and our children, cannot learn. When we are angry, frustrated, or upset, we are downstairs.

Think about the last time you had an argument with your spouse where voices were raised or anger was the undertone. Do you feel like either of you resolved anything? Likely not. If we are angry or our child is frustrated, we are not going to teach them anything. It is always better to teach from a place of composure, even if that means the disciplinary conversation and consequences need to happen at a later time. We must get to a place of calm if our goal is to enable better behavior in the future.

In fact, the following suggestion is an effective one you can use with your child if you can manage to stay calm in the face of toddler irrationality. I'm including it here because it works, but only if you have the emotional stamina to execute it.

Toddlers can get worked up in a hurry. Here's the trick: the more they get worked up, the quieter you become. Humans feed off of each other. Becoming obnoxiously calm and quiet while they are losing their minds will help them gather themselves and shows them that problems can only be solved when everyone is calm.

There will be times when you may legitimately think your child's goal is to make you miserable. Ninety-nine percent of the time, your child isn't giving you a hard time, they are *having* a hard time. Try to stay calm. It's not personal.

Of course I have, on more than a few occasions, disciplined my kids from a place of anger. In these cases, I wasn't teaching. I was in "stop now!" mode. (It happens sometimes.) When I can't get to the calm place, I find it very helpful to talk to my kids about how I'm feeling. "Mommy is feeling very angry that you keep breaking our rule, so I'm going to calm down and then we're going to talk." Once our child is in their upstairs brain, and we are upstairs as well, we can teach.

The Magic of Positive Reinforcement

Whether you talk it out together, give time-outs (or time-ins), ban privileges, allow nature to take its course, or use another strategy, one thing should underpin it all: Our desire to mold our children into the adults that will make the difference God created them to make in our world. This begins with positive reinforcement.

Marriage counselors, Fortune 500 companies, and anyone who has dealt with an overly critical person in their life knows that positive feedback is amazingly effective at reinforcing desired behaviors. Never forget to make a big deal when your child does something great. "Thank you for helping to pick up the playroom." "You were super frustrated, but you used your words. Great job!" If you spend more time telling your kids about the good things they do versus where they need to improve, you're on the track to better behavior.

Praise over Encouragement

As we talk about positive reinforcement and keeping our long game in mind, it's important to distinguish between praise and encouragement. Praise focuses on the child, while encouragement focuses on the child's actions.

Encouraging phrases like "you gave your best effort" and "you really took your time on that" helps your child focus on attributes they can control. Praise like "you're so smart" or "you are such a good artist" focus on who the child *is*. Telling a child they *are* smart deters her from trying new or difficult things out of fear of not being considered smart, as highlighted by Jessica Lahey in *The Gift of Failure*. Positive encouragement instead of praise helps your child understand mistakes are a great way to learn and should be embraced. It will help them lean into new challenges versus playing it safe.

Follow Through

Behind calmness and regular positive reinforcement, following through should be a disciplinary priority. If you fail to do what you say, your child will never take you seriously, they will defy your wishes, and then they will become very upset and confused when you do sporadically follow through.

This was my kryptonite. As an uptight, type-A mom, "no" was my knee-jerk response. Where they saw fun, I saw cleanup. And so, my first response was always "no." "No, we aren't getting the paints out." "No, we aren't building a fort." "No, you cannot help me cook." Then, I realized I was probably shoving my kids into a creativity-void, powerless hole. I needed to say "yes" more and allow them to be kids. And that was the problem. I would say "no" to something that might be messy (like painting) before I realized I was stifling my kids' creativity. Then, I would then change it to "well, OK."

Don't do this! Take a pause before answering the multitude of requests coming at you so you can give an answer you can stick with.

Natural Consequences and Related Consequences

Correction tactics (and the strong opinions and misinformation of those tactics) rival a political debate. There are troves of books and online courses on discipline. As this chapter unfolds, I'm going to share some strategies I've learned through studying and living through the youngster years, along with the advice I'd give myself if I were to do it all again.

Let me start by reinforcing my previous comment regarding the baby "lottery." Kids are vastly different. What works with your first will likely not work with your second. Some kids will loath a time-out, while others won't be phased by it. Start to pay attention to what your child cares about, as this will illuminate the consequences you'll likely have the most success with when it comes to poor behavior.

Consequences can be natural or unnatural, related or unrelated. The very best are *natural consequences*, which by definition are going to be *related to* the behavior. These are the consequences that will just happen, without effort from you, as a result of your child's choice. (Often, we moms try to help our kids avoid these.) A staple example is that of wearing weather-appropriate clothing. If I tell my kid to wear her gloves and she doesn't want to, I can engage in a power conflict and assert my authority or I can let her learn naturally that gloves prevent cold hands—and that Mom is usually right!

Here's another prime example with which many will identify: Children can often be careless and rough with their toys. If we tell them that we will not replace a toy if they cause it to break, we can leave it at that. The natural consequence of throwing away a broken toy, not replaced by Mom or Dad, can be a great way to teach them to be more careful with their things.

Remember, strategies are tools. You get to decide to toss out any of these, even often-preferred natural consequences, when needed. When my daughter refuses to let me apply a topical steroid to treat her eczema, I'm not going embrace a serious breakout involving skin-opening scratching and nonstop wailing—even though that would be the natural consequence. There will be times a natural consequence exists, but it's not the best choice. In the example of your child roughhousing with a toy, you may not want to allow it to break, particularly if it's a special gift or expensive item. In this case, you might opt for an unnatural, yet related, consequence.

Related consequences are consequences created by you, but that remain related to the behavior. In the toy example, you might put the toy away for a break until your child can learn to play more gently. When my girls can't get along, they take a break from playing with each other. If my girls do not follow our safety rules at the pool, we immediately leave the pool.

It's nice when we can opt for consequences that connect to our child's behavior as we work to help them learn. However, this isn't always practical. When our kids don't behave in a store or restaurant, we don't always have time to take them out to the car and wait until they are capable of trying again. As I mentioned before, we went through a phase when my child would frequently stand on the open door of the dishwasher. She ignored my many respectful requests to stop. A related consequence might have been to have her pay for a broken dishwasher or eat on dirty dishes. Not helpful.

An *unnatural, unrelated* consequence is just that. For example, "You hit Mom, so no dessert after dinner." These are generally less effective at teaching; however, in my view, they have their place if you cannot come up with anything else in the face of behavior that cannot be ignored.

The most challenging situations arise with things your child simply doesn't care about: They don't care if you leave the house on time. They aren't concerned if a household item gets broken. They don't care if food gets wasted. They don't understand enough about hazards to be concerned with safety rules. Many times, the positive discipline or respectful parenting tools will be very helpful. There will be times; however, when you must, respectfully or not, assert your authority.

Establishing Your Authority Is Critical

I differ here from many positive-parenting resources that say, essentially, that all consequences must be related to the behavior. I disagree. Establishing y*our* authority is paramount. For me and the temperament of myself and my children, the "no unrelated consequence" protocol led me to be a softer parent than I should have been.

Gentle reminders coupled with nonexistent, natural consequences does nothing for blatant disobedience. Our more spirited children will work hard to find out where their boundaries are. As their parents and teachers, it is our job to clearly and consistently highlight, capitalize, and underline that boundary for them. Plus, I tend to be right-brain dominant and was not terribly creative in coming up with a related consequence, on the spot, for bad behavior. That didn't mean I should let the behavior slide. My softness and inconsistency were teaching my daughter that our rules were not strictly enforced and that when Mom says something, it's not terribly serious. Speaking to your child with kindness is always a good idea. Trying to rationalize with a child is futile. When you tell your child something needs to be done and they look you straight in the eye and say "no," you cannot allow it, whether a natural or related consequence to that situation exists or not. They must respect your authority. They must stop at your command when running toward the busy road. While not an approach I gained from any positive-discipline resource, I am all about *connecting behavior with privileges*, which may not link clearly to the behavior. That's how life works. If you work well with others and demonstrate high emotional intelligence, you get more choices and opportunities. If

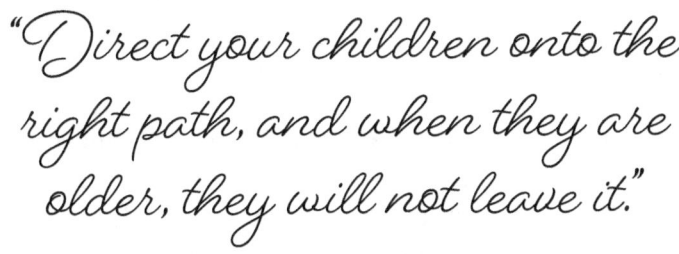

"Direct your children onto the right path, and when they are older, they will not leave it."

Proverbs 22:6

you don't follow directions or respect authority, it'll be tough to graduate or keep a job. A child cannot hit their sibling, throw a fit over dinner, tear her playroom apart, and still be allowed to enjoy a preplanned movie and popcorn night.

As we are guided to be "gentle but firm" in our parenting, I encourage you to prioritize being firm. The risk of softness is spoiled, undisciplined, entitled children who become adults incapable of thriving on their own.

Cue Up a Secondary Consequence

At this point, it will be helpful to think through your strategy for whining or fit-throwing. When you set the boundaries your child needs, don't expect it to be met with an "OK, Mommy." This includes consequences you impose or their realization that the natural consequence of their choice has occurred. Whenever your sleep level and mental stamina allow, do not backslide. Every softening of a needed consequence makes the next infraction more difficult to deal with. If they think there is a chance you might cave, they'll give you all they've got. When whining ensues at the boundary you have set, have a secondary consequence cued up.

I had a whining chair. If my child wouldn't stop whining or complaining about the "no," she had to sit in the whining chair until she could stop whining. Whatever your strategy, use it consistently and your child will quickly learn that your "no" is real and whining will not get her anywhere.

Of course, little things to us are big things to our children. Being removed from the counter to prevent a fall might be a hard blow to a child who really wanted to get the art supplies independently. Telling your child she cannot climb to the top of the play kitchen and pretend to ride a horse might be super frustrating when she just concocted a new game with her sister. Even with whining, it's still a good idea to affirm: "I can see you're very disappointed. Still, we do not whine every time we don't get what we want. If you do not stop whining, you will need to [*insert your whining consequence*]." This can go a long way to turn daily challenges into learning opportunities. It can also help your child migrate to his upstairs brain.

Discipline Requires Agility

When it comes to establishing and enforcing consequences, know that we all adjust as we go. We are new to mothering—and they are new at being humans! We are learning *together*. There will be times when you recognize a need to be firmer, and there will likely be times you recognize a need to ease up. That's to be expected.

As you teach, remember that rarely does anyone, especially a child, internalize a message after a single exposure. Sometimes, behaviors persist because the child's executive functioning software is operating on a single bar of service. Other times, they are intentionally ignoring or pushing boundaries. Try to identify the root cause of behavior issues and then adjust as needed. For example, your home simply might need more toddler-proofing versus handing down a consequence. Or, you might need to allocate more time for them (or even you) to get much-needed rest. You might need to tap into different motivators for your child.

And sometimes, you might need to double down. I'm not sure if you'll find this in any parent handbook, but I liked to use the word "reminder" for those times when my child's sleep or a lack of brain development was not at play. I wasn't punishing them; I was reminding them of our rules. If they continued to break the rules, then we must need a better (i.e., more unpleasant) reminder to help them follow that rule.

Do recognize that all kids will regress. As their brain develops, it generally does not do so in a completely linear, seamless way. They may follow a house rule for a time and then suddenly appear to forget it. I've heard so many moms express frustration over a child-development challenge they thought they were past only for it to pop up again. It's normal. Persist—with love and firmness.

There Is No Discipline Silver Bullet

Unfortunately, you will likely come across conflicting information when it comes to discipline. A key point made in positive-discipline circles is that rewards should be avoided. No checkout aisle treat for behaving in the store. No sticker chart for using the potty. No reward of any kind for progress in dealing with a big emotion. This made sense to me. Children should learn to do the right thing because it's the right thing. I want my children to be motivated intrinsically, not because they are after an external reward.

Later, my daughter underwent an extensive psychological evaluation while on the path to treatment for her genetic disorder. Our therapist noted some combative behavior, and recommended a book to help: *The Kazdin Method for Parenting the Defiant Child*. This resource, written by Dr. Alan E. Kazdin, flew in the face of the "no rewards" guidance I had previously received. It highly recommended charts or systems in which all children, not just defiant ones, can tangibly see the connection between positive behaviors and outcomes. It also noted that these types of reward systems do not lead a child toward a life motivated by external reward.

Whether or not you use rewards systems is your choice. What I want to convey is that you will receive inconsistent advice, even from so-called experts. Give choices. Don't give choices. Use rewards. Don't use rewards. And on and on. Make sure you are giving that little voice in your head plenty of airtime. Here again, mom-gut is far more effective than you might realize when it comes to parenting.

Delayed Gratification

An aspect of my new teaching job I did not foresee was punishment— for *myself.*

There will be times where you must make a tough choice in the name of teaching that sucks for you. One day, the weather forecast looked great. I was really looking forward to getting out in the sunshine and taking my kids to the pool. That morning, they were behaving terribly. Fighting, not listening to me, complaining, all of it. I could not, in good conscience, say, "This is not how we treat one another but get your bathing suits on, we're going swimming." We did not go swimming that day. TV time is another great example of how we moms can feel the burn of necessary child discipline.

TV truly is a fabulous babysitter. Not only will your child sit quietly, but also your house will remain in the exact same state as when the TV watching began. If I take away TV time due to bad behavior, I have to be prepared for the toy-covered floor, craft mishaps, and other messes to result. I will then need to manage the cleanup effort.

These are the delayed gratification days. We deal with the burden today to raise the amazing kids who will successfully navigate adulthood down the road.

Strategies for Discipline Success

I want to finish this chapter by providing you with some strategies that can be very helpful as you strive to raise loving, respectful children.

- **Set consequences in advance.** Avoid snapping in the moment of bad behavior and handing down a punishment. Rather, after your brain is back upstairs, sit your child down, explain that the behavior is unacceptable, and talk about what will happen if your child behaves this way again. Explain to your child that if she interrupts you while you're on the phone, your answer to her request will always be "no." If she waits, you might say yes or no. If your child is too rough with a toy, that toy will need to take a break. The next time the rule is broken, the next steps are clear. I liked to tell my children that *they* made the choice to lose a privilege, reminding them of our prior agreement. It's also great when you don't have to come up with a consequence on the spot when the behavior occurs.

- **Involve your child in setting consequences.** You can even ask your child for ideas on what should happen if they repeat the undesired behavior. Have your child repeat what becomes your agreement. This is a great teaching approach because it helps fill their little power bucket and gets their skin in the game. If the rule is broken again, you simply remind them of the outcome they helped to craft.

- **Practice!** Marianne Miller, seasoned mom of four and author of *The Gift of Enough*, shared this tip with me and it blew my mind. Her boys struggled with proper behavior while shopping. So, rather than going to a park on a beautiful Saturday afternoon, her husband took the boys to various stores to practice behaving. They were well aware that they were missing park time and that they would keep on practicing as long as it took to become better shoppers. Dad was not trying to balance teaching the kids proper behavior *and* get home with everything on the list. There was no list. The time spent that day in Target and JoAnne Fabrics was solely focused on teaching. You can practice in other situations too.

Pretend play can be a great way to practice specific behaviors. If your child is having trouble getting along with others, use a stuffed animal to practice kind words at a pretend playdate, for example. You could even make your child the parent and have her teach you a rule or desired behavior. Whatever issue you may be facing, consider play-based teaching to enable progress.

- **Have regular check-ins.** This is another proactive approach to let your child know their opinion matters and to instill a problem-solving mindset. When your child is old enough to participate, have official check-ins. Here, each person can talk about what they liked about the previous week along with what didn't go so well. It's a chance to reinforce the teamwork needed to help the family run smoothly, allows everyone a chance to offer up possible solutions, and creates alignment on the plan for the week ahead. I like to ask my kids if there is anything I can do to be a better mom. This approach gains strength as kids grow, but it's a great habit to get into even in the twos and threes.

- **Prepare for some protectiveness over their things.** Youngsters (and let's be honest, all of us) lean toward selfishness. This is especially true when it comes to things. You'll likely hear some version of "that's mine!" or "she took my sticker!" In my house, if an item is special, my daughter can put it in her bedroom (the child's side of the bedroom or in a specific container would work too).

Here, it cannot be touched without her permission. If it's in common territory, it's fair game for anyone. This allows kids to have a bit of control while also having to work with others to play with the majority of items that live in common areas.

- **Be ready for public parenting.** Parenting in public is hard, especially when your infant is screaming or your young child is not cooperating. You have to decide how to deal with the behavior while being acutely aware that others are watching you. Are you going to be able to stop your baby's crying? Are you going to tolerate disobedience? Are you going to bribe them in hopes of quick cooperation? You will ask yourself, *What will others think of my parenting?* This includes the presence of extended family members. I always feel a pull to be the clear "boss" of my child when others are watching. But, that's not always the best. If my child is throwing a fit but I know the root cause is tiredness, handing down a consequence is not the best solution. It will be difficult, but do your best and try not to change your parenting just because other people might be watching. Keep the focus on your child who needs your attention in this moment. Bystanders don't know what life has been like in your house. The opinions of others are just that: Opinions. They don't matter. You are in charge of raising your child and you will do what is best in each moment, public or not.

- **"When/then" is a great tool**. This strategic sequence can help kids with things they don't want to do. This works best with outcomes that can be immediately recognized by your child. It helps fill their power bucket as they are in charge of when they are able to do the thing they want to do. Here are some phrases you can utilize as examples of the "when/then" tool in action:

- "When your toys are picked up, then we can play outside."

- "When you get dressed, then we can eat breakfast."

- **Timers are also very helpful.** I recommend a sixty-minute kids' visual timer. (I found mine on Amazon). They can easily see how much time remains for a specific activity. This can be useful when playtime is over, when the breakfast dishes will be cleared in order to make it out the door on time, or any time your child might struggle with a transition. It gives the child a chance to digest that a change is coming and it makes the timer the bad guy, not you.

- **Practice balloon breaths.** When I heard about this one from a child psychologist, I thought it was silly, but my girls loved it. When they got worked up, this really would help them calm down. The child simply inhales for three counts while raising their arms overhead, and then with one big exhale, they drop their arms. They are filling up the balloon with the inhales and popping it with the exhale. This is a good one for you too. When you feel your stress levels increasing, take deep breaths, as deep as you can.

- **Give them a hug.** There is power in asking, "Do you need a hug?" This reinforces that even in tough moments, you love your child no matter what. There is nothing he can do that will make you love him less. Sometimes, this shifted to "I could use a hug. Could you please give me one?"

I hope you found some useful tips to stash away as you venture into toddlerhood. It takes a special kind of foresight to help children learn through these early years. No parent has ever exited this disciplinary territory without a few regrets. There were certainly more times than I'd like to admit when I was short-tempered with my young child. But these became great opportunities to model apologizing and forgiveness. Even through our missteps, we can teach our kids that we are not perfect. We need grace, just like them. Always keep in mind that your kiddos are their own person. Just like you must compromise with anyone you work closely with, there is now another person in the home with his own set of ideas and opinions. You'll have to create the line between required respect for Mom and Dad and allowing your child to grow into a strong, independent adult.

Remember my previous note on self-care? Hopefully, it is getting more and more clear why this is critical. You are a mom. This means that you are a steady hand. A grower of confidence. A values-instiller. A foundation-setter. A needs-provider. A problem-solver. You are the longest and strongest string in your child's web of people they can call at two in the morning when they are all grown up. Your job is to love on yourself to whatever degree necessary in order to allow you to provide firmness over frustration and extend grace over exasperation. The love you show yourself will get passed on to your child. Win-win.

The near-universal truth holds here as well—the greatest things rarely come easy. Holding firm boundaries is not easy. Teaching through repeated infractions is not easy. Skipping a weekend trip to the zoo can be terribly difficult, especially if time with your child has been limited. But you can, and will because you understand the big picture. You are now a teacher, an always-on role model, and the most important influence in your child's life. No one has the ability to make the world better than a mom through her investment in her children. Think about that. Repeatedly giving of yourself, making the hard decisions, showcasing unconditional love, and providing relentless support and guidance is the greatest blessing anyone could give to another. It's incredible. We celebrate with exaggeration when they showcase selflessness. We encourage them to try again and this time, to give their best effort. We hold a boundary to teach them respect for others. Most importantly, we show them God's love. And through it all, we validate their feelings no matter how silly they might be. Because they aren't silly. They are learning. And we are their teacher.

CHAPTER 9

Writing *Your* Mom Story

As you lean into motherhood, know that your mom journey will be as unique as you are. You bring your own childhood experience, values, ideals, goals, and unique partnership with your husband to the table. Now that you have a better idea of what early motherhood entails, it is a great time to reflect and set some loose intentions. Let's start with the big picture.

Raising a young child is a job of repetition, empathy, frustration management, continuous adjustment, and of course, love. Give and take is the new reality. Many seasoned moms have said they think women can "have it all"—but not at the same time. Raising a child is a wonderful, massive job. Your time and energy are fixed. I want your mothering experience to be everything you hope it will be. Thinking through your personal goals and ambitions, not just for motherhood, but beyond, will help make this happen. Ask yourself these questions, thinking many years down the road:

- What will make you most proud of yourself when you look back?

- What kind of children will you hope to have raised?

- How high on the career ladder would you like to have climbed?

- What do you want your annual bloodwork results to reveal?

- What do you want your savings account to look like?

- How much would you like to have grown in your faith?

- How strong would you like your marriage to be?

- How strong would you like your friendships to be?

- What sacrifices are you willing to make and what things are nonnegotiable?

- What activities light you up inside and need to be a mainstay throughout your life?

- Big-picture – what are your priorities?

Sit with these for a while. We will come back to them at the end of this chapter. As you adjust to being a mom, changes, challenges, and chaos will come your way. If you are firmly grounded in your big-picture priorities, staying *your* course, whatever you want that to look like, will be much easier. These priorities are your north star.

Now, think about where you need to invest your time and energy to bring these priorities to life. What type of partnership with your husband is needed? What will your "tribe" need to look like? What will your weekday and weekend schedule need to entail? Now let's bring it down from the ten-thousand-foot view. With your entire motherhood runway in front of you, think about your child-raising long game. As you allocate precious time and energy toward your aspirations, give the softer values and life skills their due space in your plan. Specifically, what values and skills do you want to tattoo on your child's brain and heart?

I don't imagine the vision I have for my kids is much different from yours, although it may be. I want my kids to be kind, humble, confident, resilient, and gritty. I want them to have a strong character, which for me means taking the high road, even when no one is looking. I want them to know that mistakes are the best way to learn. I want them to know how to effectively work with and see the value in others. Most of all, I want them to know the love and mercy of our Lord surrounds them anytime they seek it out. I recognize that raising my kids to hold these values will require my effort and intention. What values do you want to teach your children?

Set Yourself Up for Success

Just like every great company has a vision, strategy, and building blocks to bring that strategy to life, the same ideas hold at home. After setting our intentions, we should establish the actions that will make them possible. This can be done in small, yet powerful ways even when our kids are very young.

I have heard time and again that today's youth cannot handle disappointment. I don't want this for my kids. I want them to learn persistence. To help us get there, I've created some family rules, of sorts. For example, when my oldest was trying to hula-hoop she was having a hard time and said, "I quit." I then said: "That's too bad because you are a member of our family, and our family doesn't quit." Years later, both of my girls have reminded each other of this "rule" whenever someone doesn't want to stick with something. I reinforce this idea with obnoxious enthusiasm whenever my kids make a mistake. "Hey, you are learning! We learn the most through mistakes. Success doesn't teach us nearly as much!" Getting clear on this value has allowed me to seize opportunities to foster it. It has also helped me avoid my tendency to get upset when my home décor gets broken.

As my children get older, I hope to instill in them a sense of gratitude and a service mindset. If I'm serious about this, I'm going to need to build in some regular community service time for our family. It's the actions behind the intentions that are going to make the difference.

Intentions Come with Trade-offs

The more thought you put into the kind of mom you want to be, the more likely you will be to achieve this vision. It is totally up to you what this looks like. Getting straight on your big picture and overall priorities brings with it an irreplaceable, inner conviction to help combat the insecurity and outside pressures so many new moms feel. It's important to recognize, though, that the goals we have for ourselves as moms are accompanied by trade-offs.

For example, it is important for me to limit the amount of time my kids spend in front of screens. I recognize that this means my house will be messier, I will have to deal with more sibling arguments, my attention will be pulled in more directions, and I will be doing more bento box dinners during this season of life.

As my children grow, I want them to feel responsible and capable. This means I am going to need to slow down and embrace imperfection as I let my children stumble through the learning process of folding clothes into a wrinkled ball, stirring dinner onto the floor, "cleaning" the now-streaked windows, and the multitude of tasks I can do much faster on my own. These are choices I make with intention, which allows me to better accept the trade-offs.

Let me call to mind something you already know: the easy path is often the least fulfilling. Think about the greatest accomplishments you have had in your life. I bet those moments were surrounded by effort, discomfort, trade-offs, and persistence. But you did it, and it paid off.

Doing hard things is awesome. It stretches us. It allows us to achieve things we otherwise could not. It breeds limitless benefits. Molding the life of your child may very well be the greatest accomplishment you ever look back on. As such, getting there will include some serious sacrifices. Those sacrifices will be easier to make because you know exactly why you are making them.

Peak vs. PJ Parenting

Every new mom, at some point, has the thought: "Am I screwing my kid up?" You have these goals, and somewhere in the haze of early motherhood, you realize they don't seem to be happening. Time has seemingly disappeared without giving you a chance to teach your child that thing you wanted to teach her. Your child seems to be greedy and ungrateful. You have declined a mommy's helper several times in the name of sanity. No, you are not screwing up your child. Remember, this is a very long game. As noted in the awesome children's book *Rosie Revere*, "The only true failure can come if you quit." The more our goals go awry, the more chances we have to recenter and move forward. We get to do this a lot as new moms. In fact, there are many times we *should* take to PJ parenting.

PJ parenting is relaxing expectations, taking needed rest, clearing the schedule, and minimizing stressors. PJ parenting helps us manage our energy. Early motherhood always (sporadically) brings rough patches of sleep disruption, the emotional toll of a discontented child, a to-do list that has become unmanageable, and a multitude of other energy-zappers. During these phases, hop into your PJs and take a step back. Be free to cancel social plans. Serve cereal out of paper bowls. Trade in storytime for screen time. Re-wear clothes. Do the bare minimum.

Alternatively, peak parenting is when you are rocking your mom-game just the way you want to rock it. You are making kid-choice time happen. You are serving healthy meals. You happily stop what you are doing and engage when your child yells: "Mom, watch me!" You say prayers and read stories. This is the ideal. But, it is not practical to sustain peak parenting one hundred percent of the time. Put on your PJs when you need to so that you can fuel up and get back to peak parenting when you are able.

You will make choices moment to moment and week to week on when you will PJ parent, and when you will peak parent. The goal is to be deliberate so you can feel good about these choices. Far too often, I would oblige my children's latest request while my energy slowly disappeared along with my patience. This resulted in disrespectful vs. respectful parenting toward my children shortly thereafter. Or, I would give in to screen time simply because I did not want to deal with the push back I would have received had my answer been "no." I then regretted failing to adhere to my intentions around screen time.

As you are faced with various parenting choices throughout the day, ask yourself: "Do I want to PJ parent or peak parent here?" And remember, parenting is an imperfect game played over many years with plenty of, often unexpected, adaptations.

God Is the True Guide

While establishing our mom intentions greatly helps in guiding our daily work, we must recognize that our children are their own people. Their successes and failures are not a direct representation of us. I think many parents view their child's accolades (or missteps) as a reflection of their parenting. Never take too much credit for the accomplishments of your child, nor too much blame for their slipups. Our go-getters are going to "go-get," whether we push them to or not. Our free-spirited children are going to smell the roses, whether we tell them to or not. We are guides. We must guide them to be the best version of themselves, and no one else. As the years pass, we recognize just how limited our control really is. I recall someone asking Kathy Lee Gifford how she raised such great children. Her response, "On my knees." Keep God close. He is the ultimate guide. He also guides us to grow in holiness as we carry out our mom vocation.

As we instill the values in our children that will guide them to thrive, *we* get better. I can't tell you how many times I was teaching my kids to "think about how that made her feel" only to be interrupted by my conscience saying, "Hey there, pot." If I really want my kids to let unimportant things roll off their backs,

I should probably work on relaxing a bit. If I want my kids to keep being their best, even in an unfair situation, I should probably lay off the horn when I'm cut off in traffic. If I want them to speak with a kind tone and give people the grace that we all need, I had better get rid of the condescending tone I often shoot off at my husband. Motherhood brings with it so many hidden blessings of life-changing magnitude. It's just awesome.

Make It Your Journey

The final chapters of this book are dedicated to practical tips and reminders to make your daily life with a little one easier. Before we get there, I want to give you a chance to reflect. A wonderful vice president I worked with in my premom job once told me: "If it's not on paper, it's not real."

Here is space to make your goals real. These questions are also available for download so you can revisit and refine them over time. Find it at: lori-arnold.com/book.

Take a few minutes with each question. Reflect. Jot some ideas down. Ask the Lord to guide your intentions. This is important stuff that will take some time. As always, you can change, adjust, delete, add, and anything else you need to do as you move through your journey. These are your priorities. Make them work for you. And do extend yourself a ton of grace. Working toward these goals will include many diversions. Knowing your ideal path is the first step to getting back on that path when you run into a detour. You're going to rock this, Momma!

- What will make you most proud of yourself when you look back?

_____

_____

_____

_____

_____

_____

_____

_____

_____

_____

_____

_____

_____

_____

_____

_____

_____

_____

• What kind of children will you hope to have raised?

_____

_____

_____

_____

_____

_____

_____

_____

_____

_____

_____

_____

_____

_____

_____

_____

_____

_____

_____

_____

_____

- How high on the career ladder would you like to have climbed?

_____

_____

_____

_____

_____

_____

_____

_____

_____

_____

_____

_____

_____

_____

_____

_____

_____

_____

_____

- What do you want your annual bloodwork results to reveal?

_____

_____

_____

_____

_____

_____

_____

_____

_____

_____

_____

_____

_____

_____

_____

_____

_____

_____

_____

- What do you want your savings account to look like?

_____

_____

_____

_____

_____

_____

_____

_____

_____

_____

_____

_____

_____

_____

_____

_____

_____

_____

_____

_____

- How much would you like to have grown in your faith?

_____

_____

_____

_____

_____

_____

_____

_____

_____

_____

_____

_____

_____

_____

_____

_____

_____

_____

_____

_____

- How strong would you like your marriage to be?

_____

_____

_____

_____

_____

_____

_____

_____

_____

_____

_____

_____

_____

_____

_____

_____

_____

_____

_____

- How strong would you like your friendships to be?

_____

_____

_____

_____

_____

_____

_____

_____

_____

_____

_____

_____

_____

_____

_____

_____

_____

_____

_____

_____

_____

- What sacrifices are you willing to make and what things are nonnegotiable?

_____

_____

_____

_____

_____

_____

_____

_____

_____

_____

_____

_____

_____

_____

_____

_____

_____

_____

_____

_____

_____

- What activities light you up inside and need to be a mainstay throughout your life?

_____

_____

_____

_____

_____

_____

_____

_____

_____

_____

_____

_____

_____

_____

_____

_____

_____

_____

_____

- Big-picture – what are your priorities?

_____

_____

_____

_____

_____

_____

_____

_____

_____

_____

_____

_____

_____

_____

_____

_____

_____

_____

_____

_____

• Other thoughts?

_____

_____

_____

_____

_____

_____

_____

_____

_____

_____

_____

_____

_____

_____

_____

_____

_____

_____

_____

_____

_____

_____

CHAPTER 10

Mom Sanity-Savers

While I have filled the final chapters of this book with tips, strategies, and resources, know in advance that these will not make you a great mom. You are *already* a great mom. The unconditional love you show your child is far more important than all the parenting tips in the world.

While mothering is an individual endeavor, there are many common underpinnings. Therefore, take the below advice, stash it away, and pull it out if it looks like help. I hope it does.

Mom Sanity Savers: Baby Phase

- I have done over a dozen army-crawls, in the dark, under the crib, in search of a pacifier. If you have a passy-lovin child, I suggest putting a bunch of pacifiers in the crib at night. When they knock one out, they can grab another. This saved me hours of sleep. (I'll never forget the precious *OMG* look on my daughter's face when I put her down and she realized she was surrounded by pacifiers!)

- Change the diaper *before* feeding in the middle of the night. Eating helps them go back to sleep. A diaper change wakes them right back up.

- Put a sign up over the doorbell so delivery drivers do not interfere with nap time.

- It's helpful to have a swing, bouncy chair, play mat, or other place to put your baby in most rooms of the house. I had a heck of a time carrying my baby and the one bouncy seat I had, up and down the stairs, and from room to room, while also carrying the laundry, water bottle, toys I was putting away, etc.

- Kids sleep in cars. For many kids, a car nap replaces the vital at-home nap when you get to turn off mom mode and get things done at lightning speed. If your kid falls asleep in the car and easily transitions to the crib at home, count that as a blessing. If not, you'll need a strategy to keep him awake until you get home. Consider keeping some novel toys in the car you can hand her, ask her to sing a song, or play "shadow" where you repeat everything she says. I found myself constantly reaching back to tickle the leg of my far-from-amused, sleepy child. Around age two, screen time can come into play, if needed. This is for when your child has settled into a one or two naps per day schedule.

- Keep an empty plastic bag in your diaper bag.

- Diaper-rash creams can work pretty well. However, know that the very best solution for a rashy tushy is air. Before my child could move off of her back, I would put a towel under her and get her some time out of the diaper. For boys, you might need to concoct more coverage! For kids that are mobile, make sure their little bum is one hundred percent dry before putting the cream on.

- Quickly stain-treat clothes that have spit-up on them. This will help with sibling hand-me-downs. My child had major reflux. In my new-mom ignorance, I tossed the clothes in the hamper, washed them normally, and they seemed fine. Upon digging out some of my favorite, nostalgic baby clothes for my second daughter, I was disappointed to find very apparent stains all over every outfit.

- Think about using nighttime feedings intentionally. Many moms use the time to scroll their phone. When we scroll, we unintentionally take in disturbing news or topics that weigh on us in a negative way, further disturbing our already interrupted rest. In the beginning, feedings can take a while. It could be an opportunity to get in some reading or listen to an uplifting podcast. Just keep the Kindle or earbuds wherever you feed. Alternatively, feedings could be a great opportunity for quiet prayer time, which can be hard to come by at other times.

- If your kiddo needs an antibiotic, ask your doctor if you should give a probiotic in parallel. Antibiotics often cause diarrhea, which causes diaper rash, which makes every single change miserable. Probiotics can solve this.

- Think about having your baby nap in his crib versus a swing or cozy swaddle-type contraption. It can help your baby get used to lying flat for bedtime. For safety, a baby should not be left to sleep in a swing or anything that prevents him from lying flat.

- Anchor all furniture *right now*. You might not remember to do it when your child starts climbing. I did not take this safety protocol seriously enough. I had a chest of drawers fall down on *both* of my kids. And for what? To save a hole in the wall that would be used as a canvas anyway? I had faulty judgment that my kids were fairly cautious. It didn't matter. Anchor it.

- Put pumping supplies and used bottles in the fridge during the day, and clean them one time at night to save you half-a-dozen washings. (Shout out to Jill for that one!)

- Routines are *huge.* They will change with time, but scheduling regular times for eating, naps, quiet playtime, etc. are so helpful. Most kids thrive within the security of knowing what's next.

Sanity-Savers: Toddler Phase

- Your sanity is more important than providing your child with every single developmental opportunity. My kids would ask to pour their own milk ("No, I don't want your help!") or to crack an egg when I didn't have the energy to be in peak-parenting mode. I usually caved in an attempt to empower them, but it often backfired into a regretful, "I told you so." If you have the time and patience, embrace these developmental moments. If you don't, it's perfectly OK to call it a PJ parenting moment and tell them not today.

- One of the most brutal times of early motherhood is getting sick and still being responsible for your not-yet-capable-of-doing-anything-independently kids, especially if they are mobile. It is *horrible.* Unless your husband will lose his job, he needs to take over child duty, and everything else. (The same applies to you if your husband is sick.) If you end up home without help, screen time should be limitless, the house can be wrecked, the laundry left untouched, and cereal or food delivery employed for all meals. This really is survival. Ask friends for help even if the only friends you have are acquaintances on your local moms' Facebook page. Moms are awesome. We help our fellow world-changers.

- Keep extra paper towels in your diaper bag for hand-drying. The loud hand dryers scare some kids in public bathrooms.

- Your child will ask you, "Why?" one hundred million times. You'll find that every answer sparks another, "Why?" Try to remember this curiosity is wonderful from a development standpoint. We want our kids to be curious. Still, it can be a lot. Sometimes, I had to say: "That's where the answer stops." It can also be annoying when you are certain they know the answer. Try my favorite go-to response: "What do you think?" Why do we have to brush teeth? What do you think? Why do we have to wear seat belts? What do you think? If you have an extra curious kid, look into books like *Ask a Scientist* or National Geographic's *Big Book of Why*.

• Before you do something new, prepare your kids for it: "Here's what the doctor will do at your check-up." "Haircuts don't hurt, but being still is really important." Tell them the automatic toilet might flush before they are ready, that a thunderstorm is coming, or that the toys in the play area at the eye doctor are only for borrowing.

• Some restaurants might try to put a high chair on the side of a table meant for two. Don't let them. You are now a party of three. You will already have to move the sweeteners, salt and pepper, and any décor out of your child's reach. A two-top doesn't cut it.

• I've received lots of good recommendations from my local moms' group via social media. I've also received lots of bad advice from the same source. If you are new to an area, these groups can be very helpful as you try to find service providers and kid activities. However, it's always better to go to people you actually know. Reach out to friends and relatives first to ask those new-mom questions.

• Check the forecast before potty training. Get a little potty and plan to be outside for a few days if possible. It takes the stress level down a million notches when you know accidents won't need to be cleaned from your couch or carpet.

- Keep in mind that leaving the house the first few times after potty training is an endeavor. They probably don't have it nailed. I would have my child try to go to the bathroom before we left the house, try again as soon as we got to Target, and again before we left Target. There are tons of books on potty-training methods. The key to any method is being able to commit time once you determine your child is ready.

- When it comes to any transition, some moms like to rip the Band-Aid off, deal with a few days or weeks of roughness, and be done. Others transition more slowly. My second child didn't take to her big-girl bed very well. She wasn't a crib escapee, so I kept the crib intact, and we practiced in the big-girl bed during nap time (when I could more easily maintain my patience with the twenty-five-minute process of getting her to sleep) and used the crib at night until she got a little older. Some moms ditch the crib immediately, deal with some night-time struggles, and then move on. You get to choose your path.

- Be playful. When brushing teeth, try suggesting that their favorite character (for us, it was Daniel Tiger) is in their mouth and you need to send them to bed—I thought it sounded crazy too, but it worked for me. Or, try to "discover" what your child ate that day. When getting dressed, pretend that socks go over their hands or ask if their pants should go over their head. When my girls get whiny, I will sometimes say: "Where did my Annabel go? I miss her. Have you seen her? No, you aren't her. You are whining and she doesn't do that. She uses her words to talk through problems. Please let me know if you see her. I want to give her a hug."

- Avoid white. On you, on them, pretty much anything you care about keeping white.

- On nice summer mornings when kiddo is up super early, parks are awesome. They are nearly private and the sun is only at half strength. Take a towel. Everything will be wet from the dew.

- When you are ready to help your child with letters, think about letter sounds in addition to naming the letters. When kids learn to read, they need to know the sound each letter makes, not the names of the letters.

- If you want to pursue preschool, look at options early. Some preschools register a full *year* in advance. All preschools and daycares in my neck of the woods register around January for a fall start date, but wait lists can be much longer.

- Quiet time has saved the sanity of many moms. When your kiddo drops their afternoon nap or you need more indirect supervising time, think about instituting quiet time, when your child can play in his or her room (where all dressers are anchored to the wall) for a time. Once it's an expected part of the daily routine, it won't be a fight even if they're "not tired."

- Easter tip: Leave some of the Easter eggs empty. Those are the eggs that represent the empty tomb of our Lord. I'm not kidding, my daughters get more excited about the empty eggs than the filled ones. They are instructed to shout "He is risen!" whenever they find one.

- In these early years, we tend to lean into activities that are supposedly fun, yet end in disappointment. Playing in the snow is supposed to be fun. Getting a young child ready for a snow day is quite an effort. Most youngsters get cold easily and only stay out for a few minutes. If it's fifteen degrees and the snow is still falling, it may be best to try another day or even season. Amusement parks are supposed to be fun. A hot day in combination with wait times and a fidgety young child usually ends up in the unfun category. "Experts" encourage us to get our kids into the kitchen. Baking with little kids is a massive task full of stirring outside the bowl, egg shells everywhere, and a finished product that may or may not be edible. If the effort of these things outweighs the joy they bring, do not feel guilty about pushing these types of activities off for a year or more. The time will come.

I fell into the early mom trap of prematurely working to give my kids wonderful childhood memories. Here's how that went: It was Valentine's Day. I wanted to do something special for my girls, who were then ages three and eight months old. I decided to make them heart-shaped pancakes. Having learned that mornings with littles are unpredictable, I was quite proud of myself for prepping the batter the night before. I thanked myself for my forethought and proceeded to heat up the pans and prep the batter, syrup, butter, and plates. At that point, I needed to put my eight-month-old down to free my hands to stir the batter and get it into the pan. Of course, that was the moment my three-year-old wanted me to get something down from a high shelf. I explained she would need to wait. The baby began screaming because she was no longer in my arms. My eldest started whine-crying because I could not immediately tend to her request. They were then both screaming on the floor. As I tried to prevent the pancakes from burning, I asked myself: "Why am I doing this?!"

- Recognize the risks and help screen time can provide. Professionals rightly encourage us to limit the screen time of our kids for the benefit of their health and development. Yet, it is a tool moms can choicefully employ when we need quiet compliance. If you choose to limit screen time, do not hold yourself to the same expectations for a nice dinner or tidy house as if your children are quietly occupied. Recognize and embrace that the house will be a mess when screen time is limited – and that is perfectly OK.

- Always be yourself. The "norm" doesn't have to be *your* norm unless it brings you joy. Here are a few examples:

  - Christmas pictures are optional. You are already going full throttle with the busyness of the season. If adding family pictures to the mix is stressful, don't do it. I just picked the best picture of the year and slapped it on the card, which many times included a picture with Easter dresses. Let's be real. Most end up in the trash. The ones that don't are kept by people who love you and don't give two rips about what picture, if any, you send. Come to think of it, Christmas cards themselves are optional.

  - Speaking of Christmas, please do not feel the pressure to do *all the things*. It's such a magical season. Ironically, you have now stepped into the position of magic-maker. Far too many moms cannot wait for January because they take on way too much. Don't get sucked into the "they only believe in Santa for so long" rabbit hole. Yes, they are little for only a little time. So, make sure they have happy memories where Jesus is the reason for the season and their mom is not a stressed-out basket case trying to make it all happen.

  - In keeping Jesus first place at Christmas, I highly recommend your family get an Advent wreath for your home. Each Sunday of Advent, light a candle (artificial or safely out of a curious toddler's reach) and say a short prayer for the week. (Google "Advent wreath prayers" and you will find a brief prayer about the theme for each week of hope, peace, love, and joy.) The kids love it, it is a five-minute activity, and establishes a nice tradition rooted in what this blessed season is all about.

– A formal first birthday party is *optional*. I had never considered this until a brilliant mom shared it with me. Most kids cannot open presents at this age. They have no clue what's going on and will remember nothing about the day itself. If hosting family and friends is something you love, party away. But if the house cleaning, decorating, meal planning, prep, cleanup, and hosting doesn't sound enjoyable, there are plenty of ways to celebrate your child that don't look like a traditional party.

– If you plan an outdoor party, include a rain date on the invite if you don't want to mess with moving the party indoors impromptu.

An issue spanning the baby years, through to toddlerhood, and well beyond is worthy of its own section: Stuff. When I brought my precious bundle home from the hospital, I didn't foresee the volume of stuff that would accompany her, or understand the speed at which it would multiply. Here are some tips to help you manage the stuff. Here are some tips to help you manage the stuff. Use it (or not) as you find helpful.

Managing the Mess

One day, you will look around your house and legitimately wonder if there is one item left inside a drawer, on a shelf, or where it belongs. A years-long process of supervision and reminders is needed to coach kids on cleanup and organization. Managing this aspect of motherhood, even loosely, will make life easier.

• It keeps growing. The journey of acquiring unwanted kids' items begins at your first baby shower and grows through each and every birthday and holiday. It takes no time at all for your home to be filled with clothes, toys, papers, novelties, gifts, and the like. Have a dedicated space for kids' toys. If that space is becoming overrun at any point, it's time to sell or donate.

- **Contain the clutter.** A large toy box or bin (or two) is the way to go. Shelves are nice, but they will become an untidy catchall. Toy bins allow little hands to toss everything in, shut the lid, and *voila!* everything is out of sight. The general idea is to have containers where contents will be hidden. A few shelves are fine, but don't expect them to look tidy.

- **Assess the mess.** When your child is too young to deal with the mess of toys, check in with yourself and recognize what level of clutter you are willing to deal with. Before my kids were old enough for cleanup time, I pushed items to the walls each night so no one would trip over them. With my husband staying at work late each night, I prioritized a shower and an earlier bedtime over picking up after my child was in bed. (I tried picking up while my child was still awake but learned she was just getting everything out in the next room.)

- **Utilize your tiny helpers.** Around age two, kids can begin to "help" with cleaning up. I've heard many moms have success in instituting cleanup time before lunch and before dinner. Beware that you will have to supervise cleanup unless you want everything, including dirty clothes, kitchen utensils, snow gloves, and other items you will soon need stuffed into whatever toy bin you have.

- **Clarify cleanup rules.** One of my house rules reserved for age three and above is this: If I find something on the floor, it may end up in the trash. Mom's discretion.

- **Consider toy rotation.** Chances are, your kids will accumulate *tons* of toys. Kids can become paralyzed by too many things. With your playroom overflowing, you'll likely hear, "I'm bored." If there are only a few things out at a time, those toys actually get played with. Put some toys away, and every week or two, rotate some in and out of the play area. Prepare to be amazed by this one. If your child whines about a toy you took out of the rotation, that's great. It means he really likes that one. It's fine to bring it back. You'll find that they frequently don't notice the toys that are missing. They will get more use out of the ones that are available to them, and you will have far less hair pulling at dinner time when there are fewer blocks, puzzle pieces, play-kitchen food, pots, pans, and paper to deal with.

- **Give toys a break.** When you get overwhelmed with the number of items all over your floors and countertops, grab it all, and toss it into a garbage bag. Then, take a satisfactory exhale as you tuck it away in the garage or basement. Chances are, your child will not miss the toys. If they do, you have successfully averted a meltdown and maintained the peace because when your child remembers that "special" item, you may easily fetch it from said garbage bag. If, after six or so months, they still don't realize it's gone, go ahead and purge.

- **Size doesn't matter.** The bigger the better? Not really. There is no need to get a walk-in play kitchen (or any other oversized play item) if a smaller version is available. The time your child spends with an item is not based on its elaboration. Toys which omit the lights and sounds can really spark a child's imagination.

- **Skip the art easel.** It takes up space, gets messy, and results in over-painted, oversized, ripped, dripping paintings. A covered kitchen table works just fine for painting or any crafty project.

- **Shop second-hand for less expensive items.** Not only does this equal savings, but also, these items are easier to part with when the kids outgrow them.

- **Use smaller storage bins for outgrown clothing.** These are much easier to go back through for siblings or friends. I made the mistake of putting several years and seasons of clothing in a single bin. Then, I had to take dozens of pieces of clothing out and re-sort everything when it was time for a new season or a size change for little sister. I recommend one bin for 0–6 month clothes, another for 6–12 months, and then single bins for each year thereafter. For that first year, it's helpful to label the size *and* season of clothing included. Remember that babies grow quickly; three-month clothes for summer differ greatly from nine-month clothes for winter. Speaking of the size and season combo...

- **Think about size and season when you register.** Be sure to think through this when registering for a baby shower or purchasing clothes. I was so excited to learn in April I would be having a baby girl in September. The newborn size, sleeveless dress I immediately went out and bought was not terribly useful as the weather turned colder around the time she joined our family.

This is a good time to remember that our kids accompany the messes with tons of love, hugs, kisses, and cuddles. As our kids get older, both the messes and the over-the-top affection for us will wane. Kids wouldn't be kids if they worried about being neat and clean. Your house will not be wrecked forever, I promise. As you accumulate all this stuff, here are some tips on products that made life with little, a little bit easier.

Product Tips

Please know this is far from an exhaustive list. This is yet another area where it's not a one-size-fits-all. I know some kids who lived for a Jumperoo. Neither of mine liked it. Here are a few suggestions of products that will likely make your life a little easier:

- Get a backpack-style diaper bag. I struggled for years with an over-the-shoulder variety that would swing and fall in all directions as I put my child down, picked her up, or tried to grab my coffee cup. It was frustrating any time I needed my arms, which was always.

- Pacifier clips. *(Self-explanatory)*

- Nipple guards can be very helpful to let sore nipples recoup or to help baby latch in early weeks of nursing.

- Humidifiers are key, especially when noses get stuffy. They will be useful for many years.

- A quality nasal aspirator is totally worth it. The bulbs you find in the hospital pale in comparison to using your own lungs to clear your baby's nostrils. There are electric versions, but I cannot speak to their effectiveness. The Nose Frida remains the industry standard.

- Before kids, I didn't even know what an enema or suppository was, so I'm sharing it here. Constipation with a little one is awful. An enema, found at your local drug store, is fluid you squeeze from a bottle into your child's rectum. This is motherhood. Your child will resist, but if you can manage it, everyone will feel near instant relief. Of course, always ask your pediatrician on anything related to your child's health.

- If you use a noisemaker, get one with both a battery and plug-in option. And put in the batteries. Your precious little one will stay blissfully asleep when the power goes out at two o'clock in the morning.

- Think about a plastic bathtub storage bin (there are drying holes in the bottom) versus a mesh net. It is narrow, sits securely across the bathtub, and remains out of the way. The mesh nets have subpar suction cups that will regularly come unsuctioned.

- On a related note, be aware that bath toys that squirt will have bacteria and mold build up inside. Disinfect thoroughly.

- I somehow got the idea that applying lotion to my baby after every bath was the norm. It's not. Use lotion sparingly on infants. If your kiddo's skin is very dry, look for products free of parabens and phthalates. This is one worth asking your pediatrician about.

- When it's time for a new washer and dryer, get the biggest one available. At some point, you will have vomit on a bedspread, oversized sleeping bag, or similar item. You won't have time to head to a laundromat, especially if someone is sick.

- JJ Cole infant seat covers are awesome in cold winter climates. They just wrap around the baby carrier and easily zip and unzip. It's a built-in blanket you don't have to worry about falling on the ground or getting too close to baby's nose and mouth. Coats can make it hard to safely strap baby in tight enough. They are also annoying to take on and off. The infant seat cover solves it.

- Don't buy the "up to forty pounds" infant seat. The marketing got me excited that my child could use this seat until they weighed forty pounds. *Great*, I thought, *that longevity equals savings.* I was wrong. Those seats are much heavier than alternatives. Your child will be ready for the next seat long before they reach forty pounds.

- Get mittens instead of gloves. Children have the hardest time getting their little fingers into the right holes of gloves, and they get frustrated. Also, get multiple pairs of mittens. They will get lost.

- Two words: Slow cooker. Or one word: InstaPot.

- Squeezable bear cups (like the bear container honey comes in) are great to help your kids learn how to drink from a straw. Again, this is a pediatrician topic; however, my occupational therapist recommended skipping a sippy cup and going from breast or bottle to a straw. This bear cup allows you to squeeze its belly slightly, which teaches kids how to use a straw. Just search "bear drinking cup" online and you'll find one.

- Avoid buying fun plates, forks, spoons, etc., especially if you have two or more children. I made the mistake of getting a four-piece Disney fork and spoon set. After a few weeks, several went missing. At every meal, if someone had something the other didn't, it was an argument. Mealtimes can be challenging enough without adding this stressor to the mix.

- If you are painting the walls of your house, inquire about what is the easiest to clean, which usually is a higher gloss variety of paint. You will end up with all kinds of things on your walls. Some people use chalkboard paint in a playroom that is designed to be drawn on.

- Keep Mr. Clean magic erasers on hand. They have saved my walls.

- "Water Wows" and water-drawing pads are awesome to

take to places like church. Kids draw or "color" on the pad using a special pen with a little water in it. It's so easy to travel with and the only possible mess is a little bit of water. These also make great gifts for toddlers.

- A bookshelf that allows the book cover to face forward is very helpful. It creates a home for all the books, and allows your child to easily pick one for storytime.

- Portable potties are so helpful. After I decided I didn't care what the neighbors or fellow park-goers thought, it saved me many times. When a child is newly potty-trained, they often cannot hold it for long. When you are twenty-five minutes away from the house on a walk, guess who is going to have to go potty? Our local park closes the bathrooms in the fall, but there were still some warm days we took advantage of. The portable potty allowed us to enjoy some nice time out without a stress-inducing potty situation.

- As previously mentioned, visual timers can be a wonderful teaching tool. They allow kids to physically see the time that is remaining for a task. I used it to help my daughter cut down on sixty-minute mealtimes, for time-outs or time-ins, and as a challenge. For example, if she could pick up the playroom in under ten minutes, that would leave time for a TV show. Just search for "kids countdown clock" online to find one.

- On the note of time, an "OK to wake" alarm clock has been a sleep-saver for moms everywhere. Many young kiddos wake up, cannot tell time, and therefore head to your room even when it's four or five o'clock in the morning. This alarm clock gently lights up when it's OK to get up. If your child wakes up and the light is not on, they know they need to stay in bed. (Whether or not they adhere to this system is another matter!)

I hope you find one (or many) of these tips helpful as you learn your way through these early years. Next up, more ideas to make your life easier.

CHAPTER 11

Strategies for Life with Littles

While the previous chapter was dedicated to specific tips and tricks, this section focuses on general strategies to help in your transition to life with a little one. Some information is repeated from earlier sections on purpose. These things can be life-changing. I hope you find them helpful.

The Food-Front

- Unless the grocery store is a nice way for you to get out of the house, allocate a few dollars for grocery delivery—it's a game-changer. When my kids were little, I added grocery shoppers and delivery folks to my otherwise nonexistent tribe. When the kids got older, they were my partners for travel weekends, times of illness, or excessive busyness. The money spent on delivery was always less than what I would have spent on impulse purchases.

- If you haven't heard of it, look up baby-led weaning. Despite the name, it has nothing to do with weaning your baby off breastmilk or formula. Rather, it's a method for introducing solid foods. With my first, I was steaming,

pureeing, storing, and spoon-feeding. It took a massive
amount of time and energy. Then I heard of baby-led
weaning. You put an impossible-to-choke-on food on the
tray and let him at it. It worked beautifully with my second
child. I found it tricky at first as she needed to be able to
pick up safe foods like smashed avocado, smashed banana,
and scrambled eggs. I quickly realized it didn't matter
how much was getting in as it was a learning process like
everything else. She was still getting most of her calories
through nursing. Of course, with this or any other feeding
issue, consult your pediatrician and always put safety first.

- In addition to being an over-the-top cheerleader for
new moms, I am also a personal trainer, youth-fitness
specialist, and multi-nutrition certification holder. Far, far
too many of our children are regularly fed foods that are
detrimental to their health. I get it. Prepping food takes
time. Pantry pulls are convenient. Treats are everywhere.
Kids complain. You can make your child happy instantly
with a cookie. Drive-throughs and pizza nights can be
saving graces, but if this is the norm, be aware of how it
might impact your child's health long-term. The foods we
eat as children become the warm blanket we reach for
as adults. Being a health-first family requires discipline.
I have one of the world's pickiest eaters. Mealtimes are
full of complaints. However, I firmly believe we can find
a good balance. I'm not opposed to some ranch dressing
to go along with the carrots. My primary advice: Do not
stop offering your child healthy foods. Offer a fruit and/
or veggie at every meal, even if they don't touch it. Kids'
taste buds and willingness to try new things changes over
time. Just keep trying. A bonus to this parenting stage is
that you are in total control. If you don't introduce your
child to something (like soda), they won't even know about

it. The benefits of paying attention to your child's nutrition will pay off today and tomorrow. Speaking of food, here is a strategy worth trying...

- You decide what food is available to your child and when meal and snack times will be. He gets to decide which offerings to eat and how much based on what you have made available. Let's say you offer some pasta, broccoli, and apple sauce. He can eat what he wants and leave the rest. Don't force him to eat the broccoli, but don't offer more pasta if he still has food left. If you are consistent in this approach, complaining should wane.

Lightening the Load

When something is driving you crazy, get creative!

- When my daughter threw up every night for two weeks, I should have slept in her room. I could have helped her hit a bucket, rather than arriving at her room too late.

- At toddler mealtime, I cleaned milk up from my kitchen floor every single day. (FYI, plastic cups crack and lids are not foolproof.) It was a daily moment of exasperation. I finally put a towel on the floor under her high chair. After a few days, the towel went in the washer. Problem solved.

- If your child causes issues in the grocery store and isn't old enough to be taught better behavior, perhaps shopping time is snack time.

- If something is bothering you day after day, put your problem-solving hat on and start brainstorming. Don't forget to ask your friends. Chances are, someone else has faced this issue too.

- Flip your view of laundry once your children first learn to put on clothes independently. Kids may change three or more times a day. Flipping your view of laundry will become helpful. Rather than putting the day's clothes in the washer, assume they belong back in your child's drawers. On the way, you can do a quick check for odd smells, obvious spills, or dirt. Those clothes can head on over to the hamper. Also, clothes with lots of colors and patterns appear cleaner than light-colored basics.

- Solid baby-proofing is energy in the bank. Earlier, I mentioned anchoring furniture, which is about safety. This is about sanity. The more drawers they can get into, the more drawers they will get into. The more things they can pull on, the more things they will pull on. This isn't the time for a HGTV-decorated house. If something can be put out of reach, put it out of reach. I never emptied my bookshelf. This led to me never having the ability to sit down because the second I did, my daughter would head over and pull out every single book and photo album. The more you baby-proof, the more you can rest easy. Your mind can relax knowing your child is safe, important things are not being destroyed, and the mess is less than it otherwise would be.

- Build miscellaneous time into your weekly routine. Every time you want to sit down for five minutes, you'll be plagued by irregular, but always present, to-dos. The remote batteries need to be changed, an eye doctor appointment needs to be made, you need to return that Amazon purchase that was ten times larger than you expected, and on and on. Build a time into your weekly calendar to handle these so you can rest more easily, knowing they will get done.

- If you find you are not being the mom you want to be consistently, reroute. There is something you need that you are not getting—and it's likely more time of only having to worry about yourself. Do you need to institute more afternoon quiet time? Should you book the babysitter for a few extra hours? Do you need more clothing re-wears? A daddy-kiddo day? A visit to your parents? A few weeks of only slow-cooker meals? Paper plate week? The crazy will subside in time. For now, it's not about eliminating it, but managing it.

Safety

- Bright-colored clothes are great, not just for reducing the appearance of stains, but also for child spotting. When there are dozens of children at the park, zoo, or library, it's nice to be able to quickly spot your child. This is an especially great tip for swimsuits. Bright colored swimsuits can be part of your safety arsenal at the pool. Light-colored or blue swimsuits blend right in with the bottom of a pool.

- If you are in a group with several other families, make a habit of counting kids. If you know how many kids are in your group, you can count kids throughout your time together, and quickly ensure no one is missing.

Development

- If you have any concerns about your child's development, check with your state on an early-intervention program. Many states have programs offering a free evaluation. If needed, they then follow up with services (occupational, speech, or physical therapy) with fees based on household income. The earlier an intervention for a child, the better their long-term outcome. Again, be that paranoid mom.

There is no downside to an evaluation. Your pediatrician should be able to let you know if this would be helpful for your child and help you locate services if needed.

- Don't worry about scheduling activities or teaching traditional academics until after the toddler years. That's a minimum. As previously noted, you may feel pressure to lean forward. I bought my daughter a clock, thinking I would teach her to tell time when she was three. I was a solid three to four years early on this one.

- Raising an adult is a very slow process. I hear from parents of teenagers that they continue to work with their kids on responsibility, organization, independence, and the like. I often find myself saying: "Why do I *still* have to remind you to stop playing at the table?" Developmental skills, especially executive functioning, takes longer than we often think it should. Remember, this is a long game. Persistence and patience are key.

Connection

- For the unpaid champion moms in particular, making it a priority to connect with other adults will be absolutely imperative. I was out walking one day when a wonderful, outgoing mom came out to her driveway and introduced me to MomCo (ormerly MOPS: Mothers of Preschoolers). MomCo is a Christian organization all about supporting new moms through resources and in-person events. Your community might also have a moms' group on Facebook.

  - Step one is finding these groups and showing up.

  - Step two is setting up something outside of these groups (a playdate, coffee, pizza dinner—anything) with a mom or two you connect with. After many years with amazing women in MomCo, and even serving on the steering team, I didn't gain the mom friends I was hoping for. Some fellow moms later shared with me that they felt the same. This was because we skipped step two. Never skip step two. Also, when you chat with other moms, ask about *them* as individuals, not just their kids or their role as a mom. Most moms love a chance to talk about what they did before kids.

- The value of bedtime. I spent many years rushing through the arduous, exaggerated process of putting my daughter to bed. I yearned for that end-of-day exhale. Unfortunately, bedtime can be an anxious time for kids as they have to be alone in their room at nighttime. I ended each day with a dose of guilt and an equal amount of frustration. Then, I read this from advocate and author of *Only Love Today*, Rachel Macy Stafford, who said, "Use bedtime as connection time." It completely changed my thinking.

  - I started storytime earlier. I built in the extra thirty minutes that it took to get the lights out. I used it to talk to my daughter about her favorite part of the day, say prayers, get her that drink of water, give her a five and a rock and a kiss (five times), sing the *Daniel Tiger* song, tell her about Goldilocks and the Three Bears, and allow her to gain a little power in the process. The lights went out at the same time, we both felt wonderful versus terrible, and it gave me a chance to reinforce some key messages I want to tattoo into her brain: "God loves you. Always listen to that voice in your head."

- This strategy is critical enough to repeat: You must have weekly or more frequent conversations with your husband. You may not want to, but you *need* to talk to him regularly about how you are doing, how he is doing, and how you can better support one another in the coming week and beyond.

- Manage your distractions. Be aware that it is entirely possible to spend a whole day with your child without spending any quality time with him. We truly live in a time where the opportunity to distract ourselves, or allow ourselves to be distracted, is at an all-time high. We can't even watch a TV show without simultaneously scrolling our phones. I constantly reach for my phone to check the weather, reply to a text, send an email, add something to my shopping list, put something on my calendar, etc. In my mind, I'm taking care of business. It's always "real quick." However, my kids see me reaching for my phone all the time. We've even got to the place of saying "eye contact" when we're talking to each other to get over all the passive listening. Don't forget the importance of that distraction-free, kid-choice time. And if possible, try to set aside ten or twenty minutes each day to catch up on the texts, grocery items, etc. to reduce the slow but steady drip of things that prevent you from being fully present.

Miscellaneous

- Sometime after baby arrives, your temperature becomes that of your whole house. If you are stressed, your husband and kids will shift toward that demeanor as well. If you laugh off a toddler mishap, so will your hubby. If you are about to kill the kids, he will jump on that bandwagon and pile on the animosity towards them. A joyful mom with a long-game perspective will have a more joyful home than an over-scheduled, stressed mom. It's a lot to take on, but there is power in it as well.

- Keep a pulse on the wine. There is a reason that "mom juice" has become a cultural phenomenon. The demands we face often generate a pull to take the edge off. I'm a tightly wound individual as it is. I thought a little booze would help me avoid getting so frustrated with my kids at the end of every day. Thankfully for me, wine gives me headaches, and that was enough for me to largely avoid it. However, I can see how easily I could have let the drinking get out of hand when my kids were young. Buzzed moms are not good moms. You're a great mom. Don't let alcohol get in the way of that. If you need relief, don't look to a bottle. Look to a human: Your husband, a family member, an evening mother's helper, babysitter, or friend. Connection is the best way to take that edge off.

- Be strategic with snacks and screen time. Snacks and TV are easy to overuse when you just want the madness to stop. Both equal immediate quiet, peace, and obedience. It's also tempting to reward our kids with these things. Please know that this is a constant balancing act of early motherhood.

  - Frankly, I went too far in the opposite direction on screen time when my kids were toddlers. I was firmly against it based on all the research on how it hinders a developing brain. However, I was also quite impatient with my kids. Had I allowed some choiceful screen time, particularly at my personal bewitching hour, I may have been a better mom. And, PBS has some great educational programming.

  - On the rewards front, I'm not as steady as I'd like to be. But I know that if every good deed equals a cookie, they are going to reward themselves into some avoidable health challenges for the rest of their lives.

When it comes to snacks and screens, doing what you think is best and what is easy are often at odds. The key is to be intentional. When do you need to PJ-parent, and when do you want to peak-parent?

- Postpartum depression can affect *any* mom and it doesn't always set in right away. If you ever feel in the slightest that you don't want to carry on—*get to a therapist* right away. A post to your moms' group can provide some immediate connection while you get professional help lined up. Your precious children need you. There is a joy-filled, abundant future waiting. You just might not see it yet.

    - My local moms' group did something wonderful in response to the tragic loss of one of our moms. They call it "mom in your corner." It links up two moms who have signed up to be part of it. These moms then check in on each other and stay connected in whatever way that works for them. If this sounds interesting, check with your local moms' group about reapplying the idea.

Perspective

- Embrace imperfection. You will yell. You will backslide on a consequence. You will be short with your husband. You are human. It's OK.

- You will hear dozens of times, "They grow up so fast. Cherish this precious time." Use this advice when it's helpful and toss it when it's not. On some days of overwhelm, it was helpful to recognize that my girls wouldn't be dancing in princess dresses for much longer. Other days, I drove myself into the ground trying to savor every moment. I ended up babying my girls too much, drove myself insane saying "yes" all day long, and later had to reinforce some missing discipline. The years do pass quickly—in hindsight. But you are in the present, and in this moment, a baking buddy may not be in the cards.

- Well-meaning advice is not a one-size-fits-all. One thing I love about being a mom is that most moms want to help other moms. You need to be careful though because we— our families, our circumstances, and our children—are so different. What works for another family may not work for you. You might come across a mom who swears by the cry-it-out method for sleeping. Another mom might say this was a disaster in her home. Some will tell you with total conviction to go straight from diapers to underwear, without Pull-Ups. Others have found a Pull-Up stage to be helpful for their child. Some people could not be more enthusiastic about a specific book or mom podcast, while these resources may not strike you in the same way. Being Mom involves trial and error, and very few silver bullets.

- The strategy that supersedes them all is this: Lower the bar—especially if you're a fellow Type-Aer. You have a whole new, massive job. No way you can keep up with your prebaby productivity! Lower the bar on your side hustle. Lower the bar on the tidiness of your home. Lower the bar on your ability to retain patience. Lower the bar on your expectations of both yourself and your children. We tend to think our young kids should be able to emotionally regulate far sooner than they are physically capable of. There will be a time where expectations can, and should, rise. But these first few years are all about grace.

- In consulting with a group of moms on what advice they would pass along, one said this: "Take a deep breath. It's OK. All of it. They won't eat a vegetable? It's OK. They're 'too old' for a pacifier, but won't sleep without it? It's OK. They cling to your leg in public? It's OK. They aren't saying the ABCs yet? It's OK." Every mom will face some sort of challenge that feels out of the norm. It will differ from the mom next door, but everyone has something. It's part of the job. You're doing the best you can with what you know, and that's *always* enough.

My greatest desire is for you to experience all the joy that being a mom holds. I hope some of these strategies will help you mitigate the many challenges that accompany the entry into motherhood so that the joy is far, far greater.

IN CONCLUSION...

I Wish You All the Joy

"Trust in the Lord with all your heart; do not depend on your own understanding. Seek his will in all you do, and He will show you which path to take."

Proverbs 3:5-6

As I conclude this book, I find myself filled with excitement. I'm so excited to be walking amongst moms like you who are putting such time and effort into this most important role. You are now armed with the information I wish I had when I was a new mom.

You have a strong understanding of all the crazy and irreplaceable cuddles heading your way. You're prepared to deal with a shift in priorities, some unexpected feelings, and a child who will simultaneously make your heart burst and your mind lost.

You're ready to partner with your husband and have a detailed division-of-labor agreement ready to go. You have a foundation of knowledge upon which to design your plan as your child's number-one teacher. You have your long-term vision established, you are ready to love on yourself, and you will recognize the moments God is using motherhood to make you better. And, I hope you've gained many tips and strategies to help throughout this wonderfully challenging season. Most of all, though, I hope you know you are exactly where you are meant to be, doing exactly what you are meant to do.

You, and only you, are meant to raise your precious child. God does not make mistakes. *Always* be yourself. Do not beat yourself up over the blunders. Know that mayhem with littles is the norm. Being a mom is the hardest and most irreplaceable job there is. Thank you, precious mom. Thank you for spreading God's love to the world through your work. Thank you for your quiet dedication. Thank you for your relentless love. Let that love carry you through the hard days, allow you to relish in the wonderful days, and power you through any obstacle you might face. I am praying for you and cheering you on!

If you found this book helpful, it would mean more than you know if you would be willing to leave a review at your preferred online book retailer. Each review increases the chance that other new moms can access this "Heads Up" and gain more joy in these incredible, early years.

Want to stay in touch? I would love it. Find me at: lori-arnold.com.

You are fierce. You are capable. You are irreplaceable. Go get 'em!

I wish you all the joy and blessings,

Lori

About the Author

I'm Lori, and I had a regrettably rough start to motherhood. I could not have been more clueless on the limitless ways in which a baby changes every single thing about both daily life and its meaning. I'm a ponderer and corporate-groomed problem-solver. This led me to read dozens of parenting books and over-analyze each parenting challenge I faced, looking for a better way. I'm a full-blown, completely invested mother of two. I also have experience as a Division I athlete, MBA-trained researcher, personal trainer, wife, volunteer, and ever-evolving woman who is wound a little too tightly. I'm also a ketogenic diet guru and macronutrient wizard due to my daughter's genetic disorder. Above all else, I am a follower of Almighty God. I work and pray every day that He guide me to make the difference He created me to make during my Earthly time. I hope this book helps make some of that difference for you. You can find me at lori-arnold.com, where my mission is to help moms win the long-game.

Resources & References

CHAPTER 1

Sacks, Alexandra, M.D. "Matrescence: The Developmental Transition to Motherhood: A body, mind, and hormone shift that sounds like adolescence" https://www.psychologytoday.com/us/blog/motherhood-unfiltered/201904/ matrescence-the-developmental-transition-to-motherhood. April 8, 2019.

Shriver, Maria. "What I'm Thinking About This Mother's Day." https:// soulspring.org/love-blogs/entry/what-i-m-thinking-about-this-mother-s-day. May 17, 2017.

CHAPTER 2

"How Much Is a Mom Really Worth? The Amount May Surprise You." https:// www.salary.com/articles/how-much-is-a-mom-really-worth-the-amount-may-surprise-you/. Salary.com Annual Mom Salary Survey, May 2021.

Mueller, C. M., & Dweck, C. S. (1998). Praise for intelligence can undermine children's motivation and performance. *Journal of Personality and Social Psychology*, 75(1), 33–52. https://doi.org/10.1037/0022-3514.75.1.33. Accessed March 10, 2022.

CHAPTER 3

Millwood, Molly. *To Have and To Hold: Motherhood, Marriage, and the Modern Dilemma*. Harper Wave. 2019.

Gungor, Mark. "A Tale of Two Brains." https://www.youtube.com/ watch?v=JM-rV5oB5zk. February 21, 2018.

Lefroy, Emily. "Father knows nothing: How fed-up moms carry the 'mental load' of parenting." https://nypost.com/2022/07/19/how-fed-up-moms-carry-the-mental-load-of-parenting/. July 19, 2022.

CHAPTER 4

Barroso, Amanda. "For American couples, gender gaps in sharing household responsibilities persist amid pandemic." https://www.pewresearch.org/fact-tank/2021/01/25/for-american-couples-gender-gaps-in-sharing-household-responsibilities-persist-amid-pandemic/. January 25, 2021.

Rodsky, Eve. *Fair Play: A Game-Changing Solution for When You Have Too Much to Do (and More Life to Live).* Penguin Publishing Group. January 5, 2021.

CHAPTER 6

Dawson, Peg and Guare, Richard. *Smart but Scattered: The Revolutionary "Executive Skills" Approach to Helping Kids Reach Their Potential.* Guildford Press. January 2, 2009.

Covey, Stephen. *The 7 Habits of Highly Effective People: Powerful Lessons in Personal Change.* Simon & Schuster. November 19, 2013.

Children and colds: https://www.webmd.com/cold-and-flu/cold-guide/children_colds#1. Accessed April 12, 2022.

"Be strong and of good courage." Deuteronomy 31:6. Joshua 1:7. Joshua 10:25. 1 Chronicles 22:13. 1 Chronicles 28:20. 2 Chronicles 32:7. King James Version of the Bible.

CHAPTER 7

Meghan Leahy. "No, offering choices is not the silver bullet for behavior problems." https://www.mlparentcoach.com/washington-post/no-offering-choices-is-not-the-silver-bullet-for-toddler-behavior-problems/. September 16, 2020.

Suni, Eric. Medical review by Dr. Vyas, Nilong. "How Much Sleep Do Babies and Kids Need?" https://www.sleepfoundation.org/children-and-sleep/how-much-sleep-do-kids-need. September 22, 2022.

CHAPTER 8

Siegel, Daniel J., M.D. & Bryson, Tina Payne, PhD. *The Whole Brain Child: Revolutionary Strategies to Nurture Your Child's Developing Mind.* Delacorte Press. October 4, 2011.

Lahey, Jessica. *The Gift of Failure: How the Best Parents Learn to Let Go so Their Children Can Succeed.* Harper. August 11, 2015.

Nelson, Jane, Ed.D. Positive Discipline: *The Classic Guide to Helping Children Develop Self-Discipline, Responsibility, Cooperation, and Problem-solving Skills.* Ballantine Books. May 30, 2006.

McCready, Amy. "Get Your Kids to Listen Without Yelling, Nagging, or Losing Control." Online course. Positiveparentingsolutions.com.

Kazdin, Alan E. Ph.D. *The Kazdin Method for Parenting the Defiant Child: With No Pills, No Therapy, No Contest of Wills.* Houghton Mifflin Harcourt. January 8, 2008.

Miller, Marianne. *The Gift of Enough: Raising Grateful Kids in a Culture of Excess.* WestBowPress. February 17, 2015.

CHAPTER 9

Beaty, Andrea. *Rosie Revere Engineer (The Questioneers).* Harry N. Abrams. January 3, 2013.

CHAPTER 10

Christensen, Jill. C.N.P. "Children and Screen Time. How Much Is Too Much?" https://www.mayoclinichealthsystem.org/hometown-health/speaking-of-health/children-and-screen-time#:~:text=Although%20some%20screen%20time%20can,or%20two%20hours%20a%20day. May 28, 2021.

CHAPTER 11

Cleveland Clinic. "Baby-led Weaning. What You Need to Know." https://health.clevelandclinic.org/baby-led-weaning/. October 27, 2021.

Mothers of Preschoolers (MOPS). www.Mops.org.

Stafford, Rachel Macy. *Only Love Today: Reminders to Breath More, Stress Less, and Choose Love.* Zondervan. March 7, 2017.